Approaches to Teaching Rousseau's *Confessions* and *Reveries of the Solitary Walker*

Approaches to Teaching World Literature

Joseph Gibaldi, series editor

For a complete listing of titles,
see the last pages of this book.

Approaches to Teaching Rousseau's *Confessions* and *Reveries of the Solitary Walker*

Edited by

John C. O'Neal

and

Ourida Mostefai

The Modern Language Association of America
New York   2003

© 2003 by The Modern Language Association of America
All rights reserved
Printed in the United States of America

For information about obtaining permission to reprint material from MLA book
publications, send your request by mail (see address below), e-mail
(permission@mla.org), or fax (646 458-0030).

Library of Congress Cataloging-in-Publication Data

Approaches to teaching Rousseau's Confessions and Reveries of the
solitary walker / edited by John C. O'Neal and Ourida Mostefai.
p. cm. — (Approaches to teaching world literature ; 81)
Includes bibliographical references and index.
ISBN 0-87352-910-3 (hardcover : alk. paper)
ISBN 0-87352-911-1 (pbk. : alk. paper)
1. Rousseau, Jean-Jacques, 1712–1778. Confessions. 2. Rousseau,
Jean-Jacques, 1712–1778. Rêveries du promeneur solitaire. 3. Rousseau,
Jean-Jacques, 1712–1778—Study and teaching. I. O'Neal, John C.
II. Mostefai, Ourida. III. Series.
PQ2036.A92 2004
848'.509—dc22   2003019044

ISSN 1059-1133

Cover illustration for the paperback edition: "Adieu, rôti!" Book 1. *Les Confessions*,
by Jean-Jacques Rousseau. Illustration by Maurice Leloir. Engraving by
Eugène-André Champollion. Paris: Launette, 1889.

Published by The Modern Language Association of America
26 Broadway, New York, NY 10004-1789
. www.mla.org

CONTENTS

PREFACE TO THE SERIES

In *The Art of Teaching* Gilbert Highet wrote, "Bad teaching wastes a great deal of effort, and spoils many lives which might have been full of energy and happiness." All too many teachers have failed in their work, Highet argued, simply "because they have not thought about it." We hope that the Approaches to Teaching World Literature series, sponsored by the Modern Language Association's Publications Committee, will not only improve the craft—as well as the art—of teaching but also encourage serious and continuing discussion of the aims and methods of teaching literature.

The principal objective of the series is to collect within each volume different points of view on teaching a specific literary work, a literary tradition, or a writer widely taught at the undergraduate level. The preparation of each volume begins with a wide-ranging survey of instructors, thus enabling us to include in the volume the philosophies and approaches, thoughts and methods of scores of experienced teachers. The result is a sourcebook of material, information, and ideas on teaching the subject of the volume to undergraduates.

The series is intended to serve nonspecialists as well as specialists, inexperienced as well as experienced teachers, graduate students who wish to learn effective ways of teaching as well as senior professors who wish to compare their own approaches with the approaches of colleagues in other schools. Of course, no volume in the series can ever substitute for erudition, intelligence, creativity, and sensitivity in teaching. We hope merely that each book will point readers in useful directions; at most each will offer only a first step in the long journey to successful teaching.

Joseph Gibaldi
Series Editor

PREFACE TO THE VOLUME

This is the first volume on Jean-Jacques Rousseau in the MLA series Approaches to Teaching World Literature. And yet Rousseau's bibliography constitutes one of the largest in French literature. A search of the *MLA International Bibliography*'s online database from 1963 to the present, with French literature as a descriptor, ranks Rousseau third, behind Proust and Balzac, and ahead of Baudelaire, Montaigne, and Flaubert (in decreasing order of bibliographic entries). A similar search in WorldCat produces from two to three times the number of records for Rousseau as for any of the other authors. Furthermore, volumes on the other five authors have already appeared in this MLA series. It is most appropriate, therefore, that a volume on Rousseau take its rightful place alongside the others.

As the representation of survey respondents bears out, Rousseau is read, literally, all over the world. His influence is not surprising, especially given the enormous place autobiographical writing has come to occupy in literary studies. Although Rousseau wrote other autobiographical works, *Les Confessions* (1782) and *Les Rêveries du promeneur solitaire* (1782) remain his most important contributions to this form, which he essentially reinvented in modern Western literature. Both are first-person narratives that create a unique, intimate relationship between author and reader. Never before had an author bared his or her soul to such an extent. Interestingly, such openness, or transparency, can sometimes pose a problem in teaching Rousseau, especially in non-European cultures, as a colleague from Japan points out in his response to our survey. His Japanese students have difficulty setting aside their society's characteristic modesty in order to understand the tenacity of the Western ego as presented in Rousseau's texts.

For the most part, however, Western students appreciate Rousseau's frankness, even though they recognize his tendency toward duplicity and exhibitionism, the respondents to our survey tell us. Rousseau has relevance for young people: he speaks to their desire to live as modern autonomous individuals. Like them, he explores his own subjectivity and individuality, developing a nonconformist notion of the self in a changing, increasingly secular society. The concreteness of his life story elucidates for them what would otherwise be overly abstract, theoretical ideas about morality, politics, and culture. The example of his life also serves, according to the respondents, to inspire those attempting to overcome disadvantaged social and economic backgrounds. Moreover, young people can often identify with Rousseau's psychological fragility, his acute sensibility, and his retreat into an interior space from which to work out problems of sexuality and selfhood and to create a voice for himself.

Paradoxically, Rousseau presents a radically modern persona and an alternative to modernity. Despite his grave reservations about progress as the contemporary philosophes defined it, Rousseau helps usher in the new age with thinking that enormously influenced the Romantics. These two autobiographical writings raise problems of continuing interest in the literary representation of human feeling, existence, and time. Ultimately these works would uproot the classical aesthetic, which had been based on perceived, stable forms of the self and on fixed rules for mimesis.

Whereas, in the *Confessions*, Rousseau relates most of the events in his life, in the *Rêveries* he focuses on his last few years. By choosing these two works, we at once recognize the popularity of the *Confessions* and seek to stimulate interest in Rousseau among the American reading public. The *Rêveries* is particularly useful in helping us achieve our goal, for this short work is eminently teachable in many classroom formats. A complex writer, Rousseau does not lend himself easily to the quick overviews that are often necessary in today's classrooms: many of his ideas take on their full significance only when studied in the context of his entire oeuvre. Clearly, however, Rousseau's writings give voice to some of the major political, psychological, literary, ethical, and environmental concerns of our time. By using two of Rousseau's highly approachable texts, this volume aims to encourage an appreciation of Rousseau's other works.

This MLA volume comes at a propitious moment, soon after the University Press of New England brought out, in 2000, its translation of the *Rêveries*, in volume 8 of *The Collected Writings of Rousseau*. This series, edited by Roger D. Masters and Christopher Kelly, is already being recognized as the new definitive English translation of Rousseau's works. In 1995 the *Confessions* appeared as volume 5 in the series. Moreover, Oxford World's Classics also published in 2000 a new translation of the *Confessions*, in a highly affordable edition that will undoubtedly draw renewed attention to the work.

Note on Page References and Abbreviations

All page references to Rousseau's French texts are to the Pléiade edition of the *Œuvres complètes* (*OC*), which uses Rousseau's original, and sometimes idiosyncratic, spelling and punctuation. *Les Confessions* (*Conf.*) and *Les Rêveries du promeneur solitaire* (sometimes abbreviated as *Rêv.* and referred to in this volume as either *Les Rêveries* or the *Rêveries*) are contained in *OC* 1. With the notable exception of *Emile* (ed. and trans. Allan Bloom), page references to translations of Rousseau's texts are to *The Collected Writings of Rousseau* (*CW*). The *Confessions* can be found in *CW* 5; the *Reveries*, in *CW* 8. *CC* refers to the *Correspondance complète de Jean-Jacques Rousseau*. See the works-cited section for full bibliographic entries.

ACKNOWLEDGMENTS

We wish to acknowledge the invaluable assistance provided by Elenitsa Weld, who coordinated our base of operations at Hamilton College, in the Department of French. From the correspondence initiated by the surveys to the preparation of the works cited, she greatly facilitated our task at certain crucial times. Our thanks also go to Marie Message, an exchange student from the Institut d'Etudes Politiques at Hamilton, who carefully proofread the final copy of essays to ensure they matched the particular spelling and punctuation used by Rousseau and reproduced in the standard French edition of his works, published by Gallimard in its Pléiade series. Finally, we are grateful to Hamilton's vice president for academic affairs and dean of the faculty, David C. Paris, and the associate dean of the faculty at Hamilton, Timothy E. Elgren, for their support of this project, and to John T. Scott and Thomas Epstein for permitting us to publish their translations of the essays by, respectively, Raymond Trousson and Pierre Saint-Amand.

Part One

MATERIALS

The Place of the *Confessions* and the *Rêveries* in Rousseau's Oeuvre

Jean-Jacques Rousseau (1712–78) began his literary career with an eloquent denunciation of the corrupting influence of culture. Although a participant in the *Encyclopédie* (in 1749), Rousseau refuted the concept of enlightenment formulated by his fellow philosophes and challenged them on the very premise of their arguments—on the notion of progress itself. All of Rousseau's works can be seen as a development of this essential critique, as he posits a natural and fundamental goodness in humankind and locates the source of inequality and injustice in the corrosive role of society. Rousseau's works consistently denounce what he considers to be the scandal of a society that has deprived men and women of the basic human attribute that is freedom. Dispossessed of its primary characteristic, humanity is now only a deficient reflection of itself and must return to its origins in order to salvage its future. The best institutions (political, moral, cultural, and educational) will necessarily be those that sustain human beings' freedom. In the *Contrat social* (1762), Rousseau proposes a pact based on the preservation of those natural attributes, and he suggests a form of government that guarantees freedom. Likewise, his theory of education in *Emile* (1762) is predicated on the principle of innate liberty. His indignation at the "unnatural" political order in eighteenth-century Europe led Rousseau to establish political legitimacy on the consent of the people and gave rise to his important contribution to democracy, the notion of popular sovereignty.

In addition to the concept of popular sovereignty, Rousseau is known for his lifesaving suggestion, in *Emile*, that mothers breast-feed their children instead of sending them to wet nurses; having babies suckle at breasts other than their mothers' contributed to the high rate of infant mortality in the eighteenth century. Rousseau also condemned the practice of swaddling, which he viewed as constraining children's movements physically and compromising their freedom morally. As the author of a work on raising children, however, Rousseau later gained a certain notoriety when it became known that he had actually abandoned his own children, at birth, to orphanages. Not until the *Confessions* would Rousseau publicly reveal this fact, and it partly explains why Rousseau felt as great a need as he does to justify himself in his autobiographical writings.

Rousseau's best-selling novel, *Julie, ou la Nouvelle Héloïse* (1761), established his reputation throughout Europe as a man of feeling in an age of sensibility. His reputation would be enhanced by the autobiographical works, especially the *Confessions* and the *Rêveries*. Beyond ordaining Rousseau as the creator of a new kind of writing—which itself exemplified freedom of expression in numerous ways, as the essays in this volume make clear—these works contributed to Rousseau's legacy to the modern-day environmental, or "back to nature," movement. In the *Confessions* and the *Rêveries*, as well as in *Emile*, Rousseau underscores the positive influence of nature and the outdoors, which he continued to contrast with the degrading influence of culture. Thus, the beginning and the end of Rousseau's career as a writer merge and reflect the unity of his thought. (See also the chronology of Rousseau's life and the annotated list of his major works at the end of this volume.)

Editions

The standard French edition of Rousseau's work has been, for some time, the *Œuvres complètes* (5 volumes), published by Gallimard in its Pléiade series between 1959 and 1995. Bernard Gagnebin and Marcel Raymond served as the general editors for this edition, in collaboration with other scholars for individual works. For instance, Gagnebin and Raymond prepared the notes and text of *Les Confessions*, but Raymond handled the work himself for *Les Rêveries*; Robert Osmont was responsible for the scholarship in the *Dialogues*, contained in the same volume, the first. In 2002, a less expensive French edition of *Les Confessions*, edited by Alain Grosrichard, was published by GF-Flammarion. Some instructors teach only the first half (or first six books) of *Les Confessions*. Others may want to present excerpts only. Larousse publishes an abridged edition, which the teacher can supplement with passages from the full work. (Bordas had published a similar edition, edited by Jacques Gautreau, but it is now out of print.) There are numerous readily available editions of *Les Rêveries* published in France or Switzerland by Droz, Flammarion, Gallimard (Folio), Garnier, Hachette, Larousse, LGF or Livre de Poche, and Nathan. Among these, the editions presented by Marcel Raymond (Droz), Erik Leborgne (GF-Flammarion), and Bernard Gagnebin (Livre de Poche) give a wide and representative-enough selection.

The choice of an English translation for Rousseau's works proves more problematic, however, as contemporary scholars have isolated a certain corpus of his writings without translating the whole. Such is the case, for example, with Rousseau's political writings in French, presented but not translated by C. E. Vaughan in an early-twentieth-century edition. Fortunately, the University Press of New England began publishing a hardcover edition of *The Collected Writings of Rousseau* in 1990, for which Roger D. Masters and Christopher Kelly are serving as series editors. *The Confessions*, translated by Kelly, came out as volume 5 in the series in 1995, as noted earlier, and the *Reveries* appeared more recently, in 2000, as volume 8. Charles Butterworth, Alexandra Cook, and Terence E. Marshall translated the work. (Butterworth's previous translation of *Les Rêveries*, for New York University Press [1979], was reprinted by Harper and Row in 1982, then by Hackett in 1992. The latter edition is still in print.) The major advantage of the University Press of New England series is its indispensable cross-referencing to pages from the French Pléiade edition. For this reason we have selected the New England edition as the standard translation. Moreover, several other works by Rousseau—except for *Emile*, for which we have used Allan Bloom's edition—have been translated in the Masters and Kelly series, and the contributors to this MLA volume, unless they indicate otherwise, referred to it for translations, so that we could maintain consistency as much as possible in the editions used. Teachers who opt for one of the less expensive translations for their students can place the volumes of the *Confessions* and the *Reveries* from *The Collected Writings of Rousseau* on reserve in the library. Happily, the *Confessions* exists in paperback in this edition. An even less expensive paperback translation of Rousseau's *Confessions* is the Penguin Classics edition, translated by J. M. Cohen, and Angela Scholar's translation for the Oxford World's Classics series is good. Many colleagues have used the Penguin edition of the *Confessions* in the past, but one suspects that it might be seriously challenged by the new Oxford edition, with its fine introduction by Patrick Coleman, a version of which appears in this volume. *Les Rêveries* is available in translation, by Peter France, in the same Penguin series.

Rousseau's Correspondence

Like Voltaire, Rousseau kept up a voluminous correspondence. Because the *Confessions* and the *Rêveries* are autobiographical, readers may want to seek further information on Rousseau's life that will provide insight on what he relates in the two works. His correspondence offers just such enlightenment. Between 1965 and 1998, fifty-one volumes of Rousseau's letters, with volume 52 as an index, under the title *Correspondance complète de Jean-Jacques Rousseau*, were published variously by the Institut et Musée Voltaire (Geneva), the University of Wisconsin Press, and the Voltaire Foundation (first at Banbury, then at Oxford), under the editorship of R. A. Leigh. Three subsequent volumes contain a chronological and alphabetical list of letters, an index of works cited and of locutions, a list of illustrations, errata, and a general index of names. The Rousseau entry itself, in the index, is divided into his works, his life, the places he visited or mentioned in his works, and various other subjects; the arrangement greatly facilitates the researcher's ability to pinpoint a subject or a reference.

Bibliographies

As with any search in French or other foreign literature, the *MLA International Bibliography* is one of the first places to begin. It is available online, for works published from 1963 on, and, as of early 2003, included some 306 entries for Rousseau's *Confessions* and *Rêveries*. The *Humanities Index* is another good source. For French literature, Otto Klapp's *Bibliographie der französischen Literaturwissenschaft* provides useful information. Earlier critical writings can be found in Alexandre Cioranescu's *Bibliographie de la littérature française du dix-huitième siècle* and in David Clark Cabeen's *Critical Bibliography of French Literature* (especially vol. 4, *The Eighteenth Century*, ed. George R. Havens and D. F. Bond). See also Richard A. Brooks's *Supplement* to Cabeen. More recently, Benoît Melançon of the Université de Montréal has been compiling an impressive bibliography of eighteenth-century French authors. His *XVIIIe Siècle: bibliographie*, beginning in 1992, appears several times a year and numbers over one hundred lists. It is available online.

More specifically focused on Rousseau are *Etat présent des travaux sur J.-J. Rousseau*, by Albert Schinz; "Etat des travaux sur Rousseau au lendemain de son 250e anniversaire de naissance (1712–1962)," by Jacques Voisine; and two bibliographical articles by Raymond Trousson: "Quinze années d'études rousseauistes" (1977 and 1992). For a bibliography of works on Rousseau during and immediately after his lifetime, see Pierre M. Conlon's *Ouvrages français relatifs à Jean-Jacques Rousseau: répertoire chronologique, 1751–1799*. In 1965 the *Annales de la Société Jean-Jacques Rousseau* published, in its pages, an index of articles that had appeared in the journal. For a digitalized bibliography of recent studies on Rousseau, see http://rousseaustudies.free.fr/. The site rousseaustudies.com contains abstracts of the articles in the journal *Etudes Jean-Jacques Rousseau*. The Société Française d'Etude du Dix-Huitième Siècle published the 1998 *agrégation de lettres* bibliography on Rousseau's *Rêveries* in its *Bulletin* 25 (Juillet 1997): 15–20. The *agrégation* bibliography is particularly useful in suggesting several analyses of each Walk, in addition to listing general studies of the work as a whole. The society's web site is www.ish-lyon.cnrs.fr/sfeds.

Background Reading

There are several tried-and-true introductions to eighteenth-century European and French thought. Ernst Cassirer's *The Philosophy of the Enlightenment* remains helpful in examining the interdisciplinary connections, at the time, between literature and other areas such as politics, religion, science, and the arts. Paul Hazard's *European Thought in the Eighteenth Century* and Lester G. Crocker's *An Age of Crisis: Man and World in Eighteenth-Century Thought* are still useful. Ira O. Wade's *The Structure and Form of the French Enlightenment* was one of the last works to attempt a general overview in English. Peter Gay's two earlier volumes, *The Enlightenment: An Interpretation* and *The Party of Humanity: Essays in the French Enlightenment* complement this short list of older but solid presentations of the period. Although focused on a specific question, Robert Mauzi's *L'Idée du bonheur dans la littérature et la pensée française au XVIIIe siècle* explores a crucial theme that has a direct bearing on Rousseau's autobiographical enterprise. These works, while somewhat dated, nonetheless shed light on the problems facing the age and put Rousseau's autobiographical works in context. For more comprehensive coverage of the historical and intellectual background, consult the list prepared by Renée Waldinger for Voltaire's *Candide* in the MLA Approaches to Teaching World Literature series. To this list can be added more recent works in English, mostly anthologies and collections of essays. Especially recommended are *A New History of French Literature*, edited by Denis Hollier, and the Oxford *Encyclopedia of the Enlightenment*, under the general editorship of Alan Kors. The French, however, have not moved away from historical synthesis and, in fact, seem to be excelling at the technique. Two superb examples are Daniel Roche's *La France des Lumières* and Emmanuel Le Roy Ladurie's *L'Ancien Régime* (both available in translation).

On autobiography, Philippe Lejeune's *Le Pacte autobiographique* formulates a helpful way to approach the genre. Also instructive is Georges May's *L'Autobiographie*. Older but still insightful is Georges Gusdorf's *La Découverte de soi*. More recently, Peter Brooks has brought out *Troubling Confessions: Speaking Guilt in Law and Literature*.

Although autobiographical, Rousseau's *Confessions* and *Rêveries* cannot be thoroughly appreciated without some understanding of the rise of the novel. May's *Le Dilemme du roman au XVIIIe siècle* and English Showalter's *The Evolution of the French Novel, 1641–1782* provide good background reading. In 2001, the journal *Eighteenth-Century Fiction* made this the subject of a special issue, *Transformations du genre romanesque*, edited by Showalter.

Biographies of Rousseau include, in French, Raymond Trousson's two volumes, *Jean-Jacques Rousseau: la marche à la gloire* and *Jean-Jacques Rousseau: le deuil éclatant du bonheur*, and, in English, Maurice Cranston's three volumes, *Jean-Jacques: The Early Life and Work of Jean-Jacques Rousseau, 1712–1754*; *The Noble Savage: Jean-Jacques Rousseau, 1754–1762*; and *The Solitary Self: Jean-Jacques Rousseau in Exile and Adversity*. Two research tools have recently been published that provide, in the first case, some answers to many questions about Rousseau and, in the second, details about his everyday life: *Dictionnaire de Jean-Jacques Rousseau*, edited by Raymond Trousson and Frédéric S. Eigeldinger, and Trousson and Eigeldinger's *Jean-Jacques Rousseau au jour le jour: chronologie*. For a similar work in English, consult N. J. H. Dent's *A Rousseau Dictionary*.

As general introductions to Rousseau, survey participants mentioned *The Cambridge Companion to Rousseau*, by Patrick Riley, and Robert Wokler's *Rousseau*. A concise introduction can also be found in John C. O'Neal's entry on Rousseau in the Oxford *Encyclopedia of the Enlightenment*.

Critical Studies

It is only fitting that this section begin with Rousseau's own suggestions for reading his works. The Pléiade edition of Rousseau's *Œuvres complètes* includes a previously unpublished piece that could well serve as a general introduction to the autobiographical writings. See "Discours prononcé ou projeté pour introduire la lecture des *Confessions*," in *OC* 1: 1184–86.

As a classic critical study, the survey participants unanimously recommended Jean Starobinski's *Jean-Jacques Rousseau: la transparence et l'obstacle*, originally published in 1957. Several editions of this superb work of scholarship have appeared over the years, and it is now available in English. No other specific critical works were mentioned, however. Although we could have suggested further readings in this section, we felt that anything short of an exhaustive list, which is impossible because of space restrictions, would be inadequate. The reader is therefore directed to the list of works cited as well as to the many excellent bibliographic resources already mentioned. The books on the *Confessions* or the *Rêveries* written by several contributors to this volume have been included in the works-cited section.

Audiovisual and Other Aids

Several visual, audio, audiovisual, and digital aids are available to help instructors convey to students a concrete sense of Rousseau's life and works. Gallimard occasionally publishes an illustrated album on the authors in its Pléiade series. The Rousseau album (1976) contains a number of illustrations of Rousseau's life in its many stages. Teachers might also be tempted to look at Jean-Jacques Monney's *Jean-Jacques Rousseau: sa vie, son œuvre*, an annotated collection of postcards. Unfortunately, this poorly researched work contains many factual errors. For example, the postcard of the *adieu, rôti* scene from Rousseau's childhood with his father, related in book 1 of the *Confessions* (*OC* 1: 32; *CW* 5: 27), not only depicts an older and more elegant Rousseau in knee breeches but also is improperly labeled as referring to his later adolescent and young adult days with Mme de Warens. Thus the error of the postcard is compounded by the commentary. (We have chosen another depiction of this scene as the illustration for the paperback volume of this book.) If you do use this resource by Monney, which has been denounced by no less a Rousseau luminary than Jean Starobinski (see "Rousseau sans peine et en cartes postales"), beware of the often misleading captions and text. You might also want to have Starobinski's book review in hand, too, as it calls attention to a number of egregious errors. For other resources, you can examine the collection of thirty-five slides, illustrating the life and works of Rousseau, made by the Wible Language Institute and available through the OCLC interlibrary loan system. In France, Gallimard brought out in 2000 an interactive video on CD-ROM of Rousseau's life and works: *Moments de Jean-Jacques Rousseau*. With the click of a mouse, you can move from one excerpt from the *Confessions* or the *Rêveries*, accompanied by images of the writer's life, to another.

Audiotapes of the *Confessions* (in English on two tapes), read by Frederick Davidson, include important excerpts and are available from Blackstone Audio Books. In French, Hachette has produced two sound disks of selections from the *Confessions*.

Several documentary and dramatic films and videos may provide a change of pace in the classroom. A brief, informative videocassette, *Jean-Jacques Rousseau,* is one in the series by Films for the Humanities and Sciences, out of Princeton, New Jersey. The slightly longer videocassette *Jean-Jacques Rousseau: Retreat to Romanticism*, narrated by Maurice Cranston, was produced by Open University Educational Enterprises and can also be ordered from Films for the Humanities and Sciences. A feature-length, moving depiction of Rousseau's life by Claude Goretta can found on film and videocassette in *Les Chemins de l'exil, ou les Dernières Années de Jean-Jacques Rousseau* (1978, 1990; in French with English subtitles and translated as *The Roads of Exile*), available from Corinth Films. But its length (almost three hours) may prove too much for some students, so you may want to present short sections of the film periodically during the course.

A database of French texts from the thirteenth through the twentieth centuries is available from American and French Research on the Treasury of the French Language (ARTFL). Nearly 2,000 texts, including Rousseau's *Rêveries*, are represented. Established in 1981 through the cooperation of the University of Chicago and the Centre National de Recherche Scientifique, the ARTFL database can be obtained through an annual subscription fee for institutions. The tool is especially useful for textual analysis. You can, for instance, do searches for key terms in Rousseau's works to determine their frequency and their relative importance in his thinking. The Web site is humanities .uchicago.edu/ARTFL/ARTFL.html.

Because Web sites tend to come and go, it is probably best to do your own search for an appropriate site on Rousseau. University sites are usually the most stable, and an excellent one, Athena, is at the Université de Genève. The URL is hypo.ge-dip.etat-ge.ch/athena/rousseau/rousseau.html. The pertinent documents on this site are an illustrated version of *Les Confessions* (rousseau/confessions/jjr_conf.00.html); an interactive map that, with a click, transports the user from a place visited by Rousseau to the relevant part of the *Confessions* where the location appears (confessions/rousseau_lieux.html); and a chronology of dates, followed by quotations from Rousseau's works applicable to the time period (rousseau/rousseau_chronolo.html). This site has links to other important Web pages, notably those of the Association des Bibliophiles Universels (ABU), whose site contains the full texts of *Les Confessions* and *Les Rêveries*. Another site mentioned by a survey participant is lettres.net/confessions. A useful pedagogical tool, it suggests various assignments, such as *commentaires de texte* and *dissertations* on *Les Confessions*. The Belgian site is also worth navigating: users.skynet.be/jjr. And there are, of course, Web pages for scholarly societies and study groups: c18.net/so/pages/ajjr.html (Société Jean-Jacques Rousseau); wabash.edu/Rousseau (Rousseau Association); and cellf.paris4.sorbonne.fr/equipes/idees/index_rousseau.htm (the study group Autour de Jean-Jacques Rousseau at the Sorbonne's Centre d'Etude de la Langue et de la Littérature Françaises des XVIIe et XVIIIe siècles, or CELLF). The site for the Musée Jean-Jacques Rousseau at Montmorency is ville-montmorency.fr/musee/jjr_mcy.htm.

Part Two

APPROACHES

Introduction

John C. O'Neal

Organized into six sections, or groups, the twenty essays in this volume reflect the variety of Rousseau studies today and the different classroom settings in which Rousseau's works are taught. The surveys indicate that Rousseau's *Confessions* and *Rêveries* are incorporated in liberal studies programs and freshman seminars; in humanities courses on great books, world literature, political science, comparative literature, autobiography, confessional writing, travel, and women's studies; and, of course, in all levels of French, from the literature survey to upper-division seminars at the undergraduate and graduate levels. One survey respondent wrote that he taught Rousseau's works "on the road," in France and Switzerland, with a summer-travel group of students from his university; another indicated that she taught Rousseau at a prison for women in Rennes, France. Divided about equally between the *Confessions* and the *Rêveries*, the volume comprises nine essays on the *Confessions* (Perkins, Birkett, Johnston, Kelly, Coleman, Trousson, McDonald, Herbold, and Roulston); seven essays on the *Rêveries* (Kavanagh, Swain, O'Neal, Clark, Starobinski, Huet, and Saint-Amand); and four essays on both the *Confessions* and the *Rêveries* (O'Dea, Wells, Mostefai, and Fisher). Such a breakdown treats the two works equally and fairly.

The first section, "Teaching Rousseau's Autobiographical Writing," looks, to some extent, to the past and the sources of Rousseau's confessional writing, while the next two groups ("From the *Confessions* to the *Rêveries*" and "Problems of Reception") explore the new literary mode of autobiography. Christopher Kelly's essay, in the first section, also considers the problems that arise in teaching a work translated from French into English. Rousseau's personal approach to his reader in these works makes reception aesthetics a natural choice for a group of essays. The section on close readings (the teaching of specific parts) of the *Confessions* and the *Rêveries* follows a tradition established in the MLA series. In also serving as a highly useful pedagogical guide, the section reflects one of the chief concerns in producing this volume. "Comparative Approaches," the next division, emphasizes the fact that—as our survey responses indicated—Rousseau's autobiographical works are taught in a wide variety of classes, not just in French courses. The final group, under the head "Contemporary Critical Approaches," suggests the importance Rousseau's writings have had in literary criticism and theory since the 1950s. Indeed, a number of major theories have used Rousseau as a point of departure. (Deconstruction, for instance, as it was formulated by Jacques Derrida and Paul de Man, comes to mind.) Essays in this section examine ethnographic, Foucauldian, and feminist theories for the light they shed on Rousseau's writings.

As much as possible, the twenty essays interpret the *Confessions* and the

Rêveries as works that stand alone and not as representations of Rousseau's diverse output, although one essay (Johnston) explores their intertextuality and several contributors, necessarily, mention other works by Rousseau. While these essays are generally intended to help the reader understand the text at hand without having read any of Rousseau's other works, knowledge of his other writings is useful. For the most part, then, the essays stress textual studies rather than intertextual ones—except, of course, for the articles that examine both works discussed in this volume. The collection of essays gathered here contains work by many distinguished Rousseau scholars, including the internationally known humanities scholar and Rousseau expert Jean Starobinski.

Jean Perkins's essay, which opens the section on Rousseau's autobiographical writing, provides important background information by tracing the confessional mode in autobiography to Saint Augustine. The Augustinian narrative includes accounts of youthful misdemeanors, young adulthood, a conversion scene, and a new life. Whereas Benjamin Franklin makes ironic use of it, Rousseau follows Augustine's model rather closely, especially in the conversion scene. In her essay, Mary Ellen Birkett compares and contrasts Rousseau's preface with Montaigne's in terms of their differing approaches to propriety, to their readers, to their justifications for writing, and either to closure or to the full, truthful attainment of self-portrayal. Birkett ultimately finds Rousseau's novelty to consist in an anxious awareness of self-betrayal. Guillemette Johnston outlines her first-year, English-language seminar, which pairs Rousseau's *Confessions* with several of his other works. A three-week period devoted to the *Confessions* establishes useful oppositions that teachers familiar with Rousseau's thinking will recognize: sameness-difference, nature-culture, essence-appearance, good-evil, truth-falsehood, *amour de soi* (a positive sense of self-love)–*amour-propre* (selfish love), and so on. A solid grounding in concrete examples from Rousseau's experience, as related in the *Confessions*, helps students grasp difficult theoretical concepts in the other works. Christopher Kelly, in his essay, judges what is gained and lost by teaching Rousseau's *Confessions* in translation. He focuses on the opportunity to teach the work in English but points out the difficulties of translating certain terms. Preferring a precise translation to one that is merely useful, Kelly, an expert translator in his own right, recognizes, in the end, that university students tend to understand the importance of translation.

In the cluster of essays on the transition from the *Confessions* to the *Rêveries*, Michael O'Dea challenges the view that Rousseau's last work, the *Rêveries*, constitutes an abrupt break from his previous autobiographical writing. The author sees a certain continuity from the *Confessions* to the *Rêveries* in their lack of peacefulness. Instructors can use O'Dea's approach to help students reading both works observe consistencies and inconsistencies in tone and genre. Byron Wells follows Rousseau's own suggestion, borrowed from Montaigne, for understanding a life story: begin at the end and read backward.

This interpretation accounts for the shifts that occur between the writings of the *Confessions* and the *Rêveries.*

As Patrick Coleman demonstrates in his essay, introducing the division "Problems of Reception," Rousseau wanted to develop a new and close relation to his readers by "telling it all." Such an approach, of course, constituted a departure from convention. Rousseau broke new ground, according to Coleman, by speaking openly of his sexual life, by using the truth of nature to suggest his goodness and the purity of his feelings, and by establishing his own blamelessness in the face of others' guilt. Raymond Trousson presents a fascinating case study from the period, that of the former state prosecutor's criticism of the first part of the *Confessions.* The charge by Servan—who thought Rousseau's autobiography dangerous to public morals—stimulated others to respond. This essay, which reveals the fierce battle lines between Rousseau's adversaries and his friends, can lend credence to some students' critical reactions to Rousseau while encouraging others to support him. After dividing the class into the two groups described by Trousson, teachers can ask students either to criticize or to defend Rousseau, according to their own reception of the author's works. Indirectly making use of reception aesthetics as it has developed over the past few decades, Trousson demonstrates this methodology's pertinence in studying the *Confessions.* In her article Ourida Mostefai analyzes the ways in which Rousseau portrays himself in his autobiographical writings. The essay focuses on the two-sided representation of the author: on the one hand, as a celebrity whose name is known all over Europe; on the other, as an outcast who is the victim of a vast conspiracy. The *Confessions* and the *Rêveries* can be seen both as a response to the public's curiosity and as a fashioning of the author's image.

In the "Close Readings" division, Christie McDonald explores Rousseau's persuasive argument for confessional truth. The author presents himself as a role model for understanding humanity and as a comparison piece for others. By closely reading the comb scene in book 1 of the *Confessions*—in connection with a series of sketches for the *Confessions* published in the Pléiade edition—McDonald shows how truth emerges as a social contract between self and other. In a discussion of Rousseau's Ninth Walk, Thomas M. Kavanagh identifies chance as the source of an otherwise unattainable peace and contentment. His essay looks closely at the episode in which Rousseau describes the singular happiness he found in staging a lottery (with *oublies*, or cone-shaped cookies, as prizes) for a group of young girls he happened to meet one day in the Bois de Boulogne. Sarah Herbold offers an explanation of what Rousseau claims, on the surface at least, to be a catastrophic discovery, described at the end of book 6 of the *Confessions*: his beloved Maman has taken up with another lover. Herbold calls attention, however, to the conflicting representations of time, knowledge, and point of view in this scene—and in the *Confessions* generally—that make this work both a "monument of duplicity" and a model for the modern novel. According to Herbold, Rousseau's feminine duplicity allows him, as an author, to mediate between the public and the private as well as between the atemporal realm of myth and the temporal world of the novel. In her analysis of the Eighth Walk, Virginia Swain probes what she views as the essential rhetorical device of his autobiography— Rousseau's examination of the use of personification. Rousseau argues that when people choose to personify the cause of their misfortunes, they only become more miserable. It is better, therefore, to consider unhappy events to be the result of chance. But there is still the thorny possibility that "persons" are created blindly, as a necessary and unwilled effect of language; such an interpretation has far-reaching consequences for the rendering of true-life events. Swain concludes that Rousseau's life story ultimately reflects the random, mechanical laws of nature and the active, mechanical laws of language. John C. O'Neal's essay, the last under "Close Readings," lays out the various modes of perception (and eighteenth-century theories of knowledge) Rousseau uses, along with their advantages and disadvantages. To Rousseau, some of the modes can be more painful than others. The Fifth and Seventh Walks are clear illustrations of Rousseau's perceptual states and reveal his extraordinary resourcefulness in moving from one way of seeing or observing to another, in order to preserve or extend his state of happiness. In addition to being an overview of the period's competing philosophies, the essay can be read as an introduction to French dialectical thinking, as Rousseau works his way—not unlike the French-speaking student in a *dissertation*—through thesis and antithesis to a new synthesis.

All three essays in the comparative approaches section focus on the similarities and differences between Rousseau's thinking and that of nineteenth-century writers, especially the Romantics. Carl Fisher elaborates a paradox in Rousseau's writing that provides a good point of departure for discussing Romantic writers. Rousseau praised the public—especially in its expression of a general will—and feared its probing eyes on his private life once he attained celebrity. Consequently, he is both revolutionary and conservative in his influence on future generations. In comparing Rousseau and Wordsworth, Lorraine J. Clark illuminates issues central to the late-eighteenth-century literature of sensibility and to Romantic poetry. Highlighted is the paradoxical nature of sympathy, seen by turns as a natural inclination and as a social obligation. Clark views the response to victims in distress as the crucial index for moral virtue and, in fact, a situation that provides students with a model to which they can return when they encounter similar issues in other works of the literature of sensibility. Jean Starobinski measures the ironic distance separating the solitary walker from the *flâneur*, or stroller, of *Le Spleen de Paris*. An analysis of Baudelaire's prose poem "Le Gâteau" ("The Cake") reveals Rousseau as both Baudelaire's model and privileged adversary. Drawing from texts by both writers, Starobinski discusses Baudelaire's inversion of Rousseau's scheme of things to expose its fundamental error—namely, the confusion of aesthetics with ethics. The Rousseauian spectacle of beauty and joy yields to the image of ugliness and evil so dear to Baudelaire.

Drawing on the critical approaches of Claude Lévi-Strauss and Jacques Derrida, Marie-Hélène Huet considers the *Rêveries* as ethnographic discourse that emphasizes the notions of pity and self-love. Rousseau achieves a liberating altered state, Huet claims, only when others allow (if not force) him to abstain from any action (good or otherwise) and he can give himself over completely to a natural love of self. Pierre Saint-Amand revisits Michel Foucault's dialectic between work and sloth in the Old Regime and the Enlightenment's attempt to reform the lazy individual through legislation. But Foucault, Saint-Amand claims, neglects to study forms of resistance to discipline. Rousseau's ideas in the *Rêveries*, especially the Fifth but also the Seventh Walk, can be seen as challenging the dehumanizing notions of mere usefulness and functionality in society. The *far niente* Rousseau speaks of, Saint-Amand concludes, is elaborated as an experience of pleasure and freedom. Feminist criticism has played a large part recently in Rousseau's bibliography. In her essay, Christine Roulston argues that Rousseau's relationships with women fundamentally structure his *Confessions*. She views Rousseau's autobiographical writing as inextricably bound up with his encounter with the feminine as the site of loss and fiction. This encounter rhetorically marks the impossibility of the autobiographical project, of a life never fully recoverable through desire or through writing.

Beyond the common themes that unify the essays in the six sections, other ties link them in both familiar and unexpected ways. Not surprisingly, a number of contributors (Birkett, Johnston, Wells, Coleman, Trousson, Kavanagh, Swain, and Fisher) address, from different perspectives and with varying interpretations, the question of Rousseau's anxiety, persecution complex, or, as some might put it bluntly, paranoia. There are also several discussions (by Mostefai, McDonald, Clark, Starobinski, and Huet) of pity, as Rousseau defined it—a notion that is fundamental to an understanding of the author's work. The question of the innate goodness Rousseau saw in the state of nature, subsequently corrupted in society, also arises, of course, in some of these essays (Kavanagh and Starobinski). Saint Augustine's work forms the backdrop not just for the essay dedicated to the subject (Perkins) but for others as well (Kelly and Coleman); another contributor (Wells) pursues the related confessional mode of writing. And the interaction between the public and the private spheres of Rousseau's life receives attention in four essays (Wells, Mostefai, McDonald, and Fisher).

Strong claims emerge clearly, in several essays, for at least two goals or results of Rousseau's autobiographical writing: a justification of his life and a state of repose or inaction. That Rousseau wrote the *Confessions* and the *Rêveries* to justify himself (Birkett, O'Dea, Wells, Coleman, and Mostefai), however, does not need to be qualified as much as the claim that Rousseau, either voluntarily or involuntarily, came to avoid activity and to seek a state of inaction (O'Dea, Swain, Clark, Huet, and Saint-Amand). These authors may be linked with, if not exactly read against, three others (Wells, Mostefai, and O'Neal). The specific focus of one essay, intertextuality (Johnston), becomes an important reading strategy for other contributors (Kelly and McDonald). Three essays (Kavanagh, Swain, and O'Neal) independently find the notion of chance central to Rousseau's thinking, which privileges immediate sensory experience (see also Herbold). The authors of two essays (Herbold and Roulston) define the emerging novel as centrally tied to feminist or feminine concerns. For two others (Birkett and Clark), as well as Herbold in a possibly related claim, Rousseau points, in his autobiographical writings, to modernity itself.

What ultimately becomes the key tool in unlocking the depths of Rousseau's meaning on most of these subjects is, however—as Wells observes—students' own experiences. As these essays demonstrate, if Rousseau continues to speak to our innermost souls, he does so because we recognize in him a kindred, well-nigh-universal human spirit.

The Confessional Mode in Autobiography: Saint Augustine, Rousseau, and Benjamin Franklin

Jean Perkins

It is generally acknowledged that Saint Augustine was the first writer in Western literature to use the confessional mode in his autobiography. Augustine's account of his life—from misspent youth through sudden conversion to Christianity, followed by baptism and a new life, enclosed in the grace of God— becomes a model for future practitioners of this approach to the narrative of one's life.. Rousseau is the most prominent of many authors who emulated Augustine in developing their narrative structure, and even Benjamin Franklin's *Autobiography* uses the Augustinian narrative paradigm.

Saint Augustine

Augustine was in his mid-forties when he wrote his *Confessions*, some ten years after his conversion to Christianity. As noted in the introduction to his translation of the work, Henry Chadwick writes:

> The *Confessions* is a polemical work, at least as much a self-vindication as an admission of mistakes. The very title carries a conscious double meaning, of confession as praise as well as confession as acknowledgment of faults. And its form is extraordinary—a prose-poem addressed

to God, intended to be overheard by anxious and critical fellow-Christians.   (ix)

In creating a genre, Augustine had little to draw on. The great biblical conversion scene, of course, occurs in Acts, when Saul is converted on the road to Damascus. This episode is recounted three times in Acts (9.3–18; 22.6–16; 26.12–23), with slight variations, but the central features do not vary: Saul and his companions are devastated by a sudden blinding light, and Saul alone hears a voice calling out to him, announcing itself as "Jesus of Nazareth," and telling him to go to Damascus for further instructions. Saul is baptized as Paul, and thus begins his ministry in the church. Augustine incorporates the voice but does not keep the blinding light. His baptism, which occurs in his thirty-third year, is followed by an ecstatic vision of eternity. He is thus born into a life bathed in the grace of God through Jesus Christ.

The road to this miraculous conversion is long and rocky, as the following episodes reveal.

Youthful Misdemeanors

In these incidents, the young protagonist leads other adolescents into mischief. The best known, the theft of some fruit, occurs when he is sixteen: "I and a gang of naughty adolescents set off late at night. . . . We carried off a huge load of pears. But they were not for our feasts but merely to throw to the pigs. Even if we ate a few, our pleasure lay in doing what was not allowed" (29). In accordance with his theological position, which stressed the unworthiness of man in the absence of God's grace, Augustine underlines the wickedness that motivated him as an adolescent.

Young Adulthood

This stage on the road to conversion represents, for Augustine, a period of turmoil, both mental and spiritual, while he was living in a luxurious, frivolous, and corrupt society. He portrays himself as a greedy, ambitious young man, beset by sexual desires. He is tempted by the Manichean doctrine, which he eventually rejects after coming under the influence of Bishop Ambrose and a group of Neoplatonists.

Conversion Scene

In physical, mental, moral, and spiritual misery, Augustine, accompanied by his friend Alypius, goes into the garden of his lodgings. Overcome by weeping, he leaves his friend and throws himself down "under a certain fig tree" (152); allowing the tears to flow freely, he cries out, "Why not now? Why not an end to my impure life in this very hour? . . . suddenly I heard a voice from the nearby house chanting . . . and repeating over and over again 'Pick up and read, pick up and read' " (152). Picking up his copy of Saint Paul's Epistle to the Romans, he opens it at random at a passage (13: 13–14) that concludes "put on the Lord Jesus Christ and make no provision for the flesh in its lusts." "At once," Augustine continues, "with the last words of this sentence, it was as if a light of relief from all anxiety flooded into my heart. All the shadows of doubt were dispelled" (153). He immediately shares his revelation with Alypius, who finds inspiration in another text, and the two make plans to be baptized.

New Life

The conversion took place in July 386, and Augustine, along with his son and his friend Alypius, was baptized by Ambrose the next year at Easter, in accordance with church doctrine of the period. As a result of the joy and peace of his new life, he forsakes his career as a rhetorician. An ecstatic vision he shares with his mother, Monica, symbolizes his insight into the will of God: "For to exist in the past or in the future is no property of the eternal. And while we talked and panted after it, we touched it in some small degree by a moment of total concentration of the heart" (171). The death of Monica shortly thereafter ends the autobiographical section of Augustine's *Confessions*.

Rousseau

The relation of Rousseau's *Confessions* to those of Augustine has been a matter of much debate. Most editors and critics of Augustine derisively dismiss any similarities. Chadwick is no exception: "Like Rousseau's book with the same title (but otherwise having little in common), the work has a perennial power to speak" (ix). Rousseau's commentators join in this chorus, but from a substantially different point of view. The editors of the English edition of Rousseau's works are explicit: "The most obvious target of the *Confessions* is its most famous predecessor, the *Confessions* of Saint Augustine. . . . his ultimate choice of title indicates his intention to replace his predecessor and make his book into *the* Confessions" (5: xxi). In her work, Ann Hartle gives a detailed account of Rousseau's argument with Augustine. The major difference lies in their views of human nature.

Brought up in Geneva, where Calvinist theology stemmed directly from Augustine, Rousseau was well aware of the doctrine of original sin, which denies to human beings any moral or spiritual worth unless they are redeemed by the grace of God. As Rousseau matured, he came to diametrically opposite conclusions: in his philosophy, the natural goodness of humankind is corrupted by society. Despite his denial of the Augustinian doctrines of original sin, predestination, and God's grace as the only saving factor, Rousseau modeled his autobiography on the Augustinian narrative.

Youthful Misdemeanors

Rousseau gives a loving account of his early childhood, spent in the company of his father. When his father is forced to leave Geneva, the ten-year-old boy is put *en pension*, along with his cousin, at the country home of Pastor Lambercier and his sister. Rousseau sums up his impressions of this idyllic sojourn at Bossey: "La simplicité de cette vie champêtre me fit un bien d'un prix inestimable en ouvrant mon cœur à l'amitié" (13) ("The simplicity of that rural life did me a good of inestimable value by opening my heart to friendship" [11]). Unfortunately, after about two years, both Jean-Jacques and his cousin are punished unjustly, and, having lost their childish innocence, they are forced to return to Geneva (20 [18]).

Rousseau chooses this moment in his narrative to recount a humorous incident: "O vous, lecteurs curieux de la grande histoire du noyer de la terrasse, écoutez-en l'horrible tragedie, et vous abstenez de frémir, si vous pouvez" (22) ("Oh you, readers curious about the great history of the walnut tree on the terrace, listen to its horrible tragedy, and refrain from shuddering, if you can" [19]). The tragicomic tone is sustained throughout this episode, which recounts the successful efforts of the boys to deflect water from the tree to their own plant. Significantly, Rousseau places this misdemeanor in his childhood, and, of course, he does not dwell on the wickedness of such childish pranks. On the contrary, the two boys are proud of their achievement, and Pastor Lambercier enjoys a good laugh over their exploit.

Young Adulthood

Rousseau's account of his apprenticeship with an engraver emphasizes his master's tyranny, which forced the adolescent into theft and deception. Before he reaches Paris in 1742, he has experienced happiness with Mme de Warens and acute disappointments, primarily in his attempts to become a musician. In Paris and Venice (1743–44) the young Rousseau suffers further disillusionment. His quarrel with his employer in Venice, in which Rousseau is in the right but is not recognized as such, gives him the first inkling of his coming revelation: "La justice et l'inutilité de mes plaintes me laissérent dans l'ame un germe d'indignation contre nos sotes institutions civiles" (327) ("The justice and uselessness of my complaints left a seed of indignation in my soul against our foolish civil institutions" [274]). Thus his stay in two corrupt societies, Venice and Paris, brings him to the cusp of discovery.

Conversion Scene

Narrated in book 8 (written in 1769), the scene had taken place twenty years before. As Rousseau points out, he wrote a more detailed account of the event much earlier, in 1762, in the second of his *Lettres à Malesherbes* (*OC* 1: 1134–38; *CW* 5: 574–77). When his good friend Diderot is imprisoned at Vincennes,

Rousseau is devastated. As soon as visitors are allowed, he makes the long, hot journey on foot every other day. During one of the many rest stops on these walks, he experiences his revelation. Here are the points of convergence with the Augustinian model:

> separated from a close friend
> lying down in the shade of a tree
> reading a serendipitous passage from a text
> shedding tears
> undergoing a sudden revelation of the truth
> sharing his vision with a friend, who encourages him to pursue these
>   insights

The miraculous nature of this conversion is succinctly told: "A l'instant de cette lecture je vis un autre univers et je devins un autre homme" (351) ("At the moment of that reading I saw another universe and I became another man" [294]).

With Diderot's encouragement, Rousseau then writes his first *Discours*, on the sciences and the arts, in which he arrives at two contradictory conclusions. On the one hand, he describes the rest of his life as full of misery and misfortune: "Je le fis, et dès cet instant je fus perdu. Tout le reste de ma vie et de mes malheurs fut l'effet inévitable de cet instant d'égarement" ("I did so, and from that instant I was lost. All the rest of my life and misfortunes was the inevitable effect of that instant of aberration"). On the other hand, he stresses the insights he reached that he tried to incorporate into this prize-winning essay: "Toutes mes petites passions furent étouffées par l'enthousiasme de la vérité, de la liberté, de la vertu" (351) ("All my passions were stifled by enthusiasm for truth, for freedom, for virtue" [295]). Claiming that these ideas sustained him for the next four or five years, Rousseau returns to the theme of his misfortunes—a motif that becomes increasingly prominent in the remaining books of the *Confessions*.

New Life

On learning that his first *Discours* has won an academic prize at Dijon, Rousseau is motivated to take stock of his life, and he makes a momentous commitment: "d'être libre et vertueux, au dessus de la fortune et de l'opinion, et de se suffire à soi-même" (356) ("to be free and virtuous, above fortune and opinion, and to suffice to oneself" [298]). To become independent, Rousseau decides to make a living by copying music. A life-altering decision comes shortly after the successful presentation of the short opera *Le Devin du village* before the king at Fontainebleau. When he is informed that he should present himself at court to receive a pension from the king, Rousseau leaves Fontainebleau, thus forfeiting the pension but ensuring his independence.

To demonstrate his disdain for Parisian society, Rousseau finally accepts Mme d'Epinay's invitation to live on her estate, the Hermitage. There he writes *La Nouvelle Héloïse*, but his tranquil retreat is soon disrupted by his quarrel with his hostess. The rest of his life he spends moving from one place of exile to another as his feelings of persecution grow ever more intense.

Benjamin Franklin

There is no evidence that Benjamin Franklin read Rousseau, but he must have known that Rousseau had written a controversial autobiography. Franklin arrived in Paris in 1776, six years after Rousseau's much-publicized reading of the first part of the *Confessions*. The first part of Franklin's *Autobiography* was written in 1771, while he was living in London The work takes the form of a letter to his son; although far from confessional, it manages to use the Augustinian narrative structure.

Youthful Misdemeanors

A leader among his playmates, young Benjamin shows them how to construct a wharf from stones "borrowed" from a nearby building site. The incident is handled ironically, as Franklin compares the boys to a colony of ants: "we worked diligently like so many emmets, sometimes two or three to a stone" (23). Even after being reprimanded by his father, Benjamin argues the utility of his exploit.

Young Adulthood

The seventeen-year-old Benjamin enters Philadelphia dirty, tired, and hungry (38–39), but by dint of hard work establishes himself as one of the best printers in the city.

Conversion Scene

Franklin manipulates the basic narrative structure, but it is still discernible:

> estranged from a friend, a Presbyterian minister (92)
> inspired by the minister's misinterpretation of a biblical text (93)
> motivated to formulate his scheme of moral perfection (twelve virtues
>   to be practiced weekly in rotation)

The episode is related in a partly serious, partly ironic tone, ending in the latter. When a Quaker friend "kindly informed [him] that [he] was generally thought proud" (103), Franklin promptly added *humility* to his list but confesses that although he never achieved the reality of this virtue, he managed to do a good job on its appearance: "For even if I could conceive that I had completely overcome it, I should probably be proud of my humility" (104). This episode ends part 2; part 3 is a straightforward account of his business success, his public service, and his scientific interests up to the eve of the American Revolution. No further mention is made of the scheme for moral perfection.

The three autobiographies have quite different purposes: Augustine's, written when he was in his forties, is addressed to God and is intended to encourage other Christians in their faith; Rousseau's, written in his fifties, is a self-justifying vindication of his own life; Franklin's, written in his sixties and seventies and ostensibly addressed to his son, is intended to serve as a model for a younger generation of Americans. Augustine invented the narrative structure, which, despite their different intentions, both Rousseau and Franklin found appropriate to their needs in narrating their lives.

Comparing Prefaces:
Rousseau versus Montaigne

Mary Ellen Birkett

What are we to make of the boast that opens the preface or prologue to Rousseau's *Confessions* (1782): "Voici le seul portrait d'homme, peint exactement d'après nature et dans toute sa vérité, qui existe et qui probablement existera jamais" (3) ("Here is the only portrait of a man, painted exactly according to nature and in all its truth, that exists and that will probably ever exist" [3])?

One way to evaluate Rousseau's claim to uniqueness is to compare this preface with the prologue of an earlier autobiography, Montaigne's *Essais* (1580, 1582, 1587) (*Essays*, in *Complete Works* [2]). Because both passages are less than three hundred words long, they are ideal for in-class close reading. Rousseau's place in the tradition of writing the self comes more clearly into focus as we ask the following questions of both prefaces: How does the autobiographer present the "I" who is writer, narrator, and subject of his life story? For whom does he write? How does he justify his autobiographical enterprise? And how does he define writing the self?

Proper Names and Impropriety

Montaigne clearly identifies the "I" of the *Essais*. The inscription "de Montaigne" at the end of his preface, "To the Reader," situates the subject of autobiography among the power elite of sixteenth-century France. The name "de Montaigne"—equated with place (and therefore with land ownership) and with lineage (like his father before him, Montaigne was a prominent member of government in the Bordeaux region)—legitimates the ego behind the "I." The proper name confirms the properness of Montaigne's using his aristocratic, socially valued "I" as "the matter of [his] book."

Montaigne writes, however, not to enhance his worldly "glory" (471; 2.16); in fact, he finds his "powers" inadequate to that task. He places greater value on possessions that explain his character: "my relatives and friends," "my habits and temperament," "my defects," and, of course, "my book." Furthermore, Montaigne expresses the intention of presenting himself in a "domestic" and "private" light, in his "simple, natural, ordinary fashion." Montaigne equates the attribute "natural" with a "fashion," or style, defined by what it lacks: "straining and artifice" and "a studied posture." Yet because Michel de Montaigne, magistrate and mayor of Bordeaux, has not "been placed among those nations which are said to live still in the sweet freedom of nature's first laws," "respect for the public" keeps him from portraying himself "entire and wholly naked." When Montaigne notes that his autobiography presents "my natural form," he implies that the "I" of the *Essais* submits to the demands of propriety.

Rousseau, in contrast, rejects propriety from the outset. By not naming the "I" of the *Confessions* in its preface, he proudly defies social attitudes that consider it presumptuous for a man of common birth (6 [5]) to write about himself as if he were the equal of kings, generals, or statesmen (9 [8]). Moreover, the life about which Rousseau writes is full of improprieties: the iconoclastic ideas of the first and second *Discours* (1750 and 1755), *Emile* (1762), and the *Contrat social* (1762); the scandal of his unconventional private life with Thérèse (330–33 [278–80]); and the abandonment of his five children to an orphanage (356–59 [299–301]).

Rousseau does not write the *Confessions* to perpetuate the notoriety of his name, however. As he notes in the preface to this work (3 [3]), he writes to redefine the identity of his "I" in terms of what he owns (cf. *Mon Portrait* in *OC* 1: 1128): "ma destinée" ("my destiny"), "ma confiance" ("my trust"), "mes malheurs" ("my misfortunes"), "ma mémoire" ("my memory"), "mon caractére" ("my character"), "mes ennemis" ("my enemies"), "ma cendre" ("my ashes"). These seven possessions constitute Rousseau's patrimony, and its emotional richness outweighs all other assessments of personal worth. An allusion to the most valuable of all Rousseau's belongings closes the preface to the *Confessions*, as the writer refers to himself as "un homme qui n'en [du mal] a jamais fait, ou voulu faire" ("a man who has never done, or wished to do, any [evil]"). The unequivocal "jamais" ("never") recalls the preface's peremptory opening sentence, in which Rousseau presents his autobiography as "the only portrait," "exactly according to nature," "in all its truth." The absolutes "never," "only," "exactly," and "all" liken "nature" to "truth" and both to the unspoken quality of innocence that is the most precious asset of the "I." Shaped by intention as well as by deed ("fait, ou voulu faire" ["done, or wished to do"]), this purity of heart, like the identity with which it is equated, is self-evident to Rousseau. But for the "I" to be certain that its blamelessness is evident to others, this fundamental innocence—like the name Rousseau—must be pronounced by readers of the *Confessions* (175 [146–47]).

Friend or Foe?

The opening words of Montaigne's prologue ("This book was written in good faith, reader") forthrightly address the public for whom Montaigne writes, and soon Montaigne establishes an easy familiarity with his readership, whom he defines as "my relatives and friends." This circle of supporters—into which the intimate "tu" and "ton" ("you," "your") pull the present-day reader—are busy people who know the value of leisure and are capable of distinguishing between fruitful and vain pursuits. They are, in short, much like Montaigne himself. Montaigne has no need to resolve the contradiction of inviting others to read him while at the same time showing indifference to their doing so, because his first and most important reader is himself:

> If no one reads me, have I wasted my time, entertaining myself for so many idle hours with such useful and agreeable thoughts? In modeling this figure upon myself, I have had to fashion and compose myself so often to bring myself out, that the model itself has to some extent grown firm and taken shape.   (505; 2.18)

Rousseau's preface (3 [3]), in contrast, begins by ignoring the reader's presence. When Rousseau's "I" does speak to a "you" in the sentences that follow, it is as to a faceless stranger ("Qui que vous soyez" ["Whoever you may be"]); a forbidding judge ("l'arbitre du sort de ce cahier" ["the arbiter of the fate of this notebook"]); or an even more forbidding enemy ("un de ces ennemis implacables" ["one of these implacable enemies"]). Rousseau writes the *Confessions* for a reader all too ready to do "cruelle injustice" ("cruel injustice"), to be "malfaisant et vindicatif" ("harmful and vindictive"), and to seek "vengeance." But because this antagonistic reader has "entrailles" ("innermost emotions"), Rousseau deems him capable of becoming "genereux et bon" ("generous and good")—in other words, like Rousseau himself. What should bring Rousseau's opponent "nobly to bear witness" to the true value of Rousseau's "I" will be the content and style of the *Confessions*. The only present tense, active verb of the preface having "je" for its subject sums up the relationship between "I" and "you" in the autobiography: "je vous conjure" ("I beg you"). This formal but desperate appeal, whose result Rousseau will never know, ties him to his reader in a relationship fraught with need, conflict, and uncertainty.

Rationales for Writing

Montaigne's work, "written in good faith," is an intellectual, bookish autobiography (274; 2.6). Montaigne uses existing texts—both those composed by other writers, especially those of antiquity, and those he himself penned—as sounding boards for his ideas. In this way, he "essays"—that is, tests, or tries out—what he believes (611; 3.2). Montaigne asks the reader to extend "good faith," or trust, in accepting the idea that one man's subjective probing can have value for others. Although he claims to write only to discover who he is (109; 1.26, 109), his self-portrayal is validated by the Renaissance interest in the advancement of knowledge about all of humankind (611; 3.2).

Rousseau, too, suggests humanistic justification for writing his life: his autobiography will serve as the "prémiére piéce de comparaison pour l'étude des hommes" ("the first piece of comparison for the study of men"). But even as Rousseau invokes the practical knowledge that humankind may derive from the *Confessions*, "un ouvrage unique et utile" (3) ("a unique and useful work" [3]), the "unique" quality comes before the "useful" quality and separates Rousseau from the rest of the human race. The principal justification for Rousseau's self-portrayal, then, is the unshakable sentiment of his singularity. In the preface to the *Confessions*, "portrait," "notebook," and "monument" figuratively represent the multiple forms through which he seeks to project this individuality "exactement d'après nature" ("exactly according to nature"). Rousseau defends portrayal of himself on the grounds that because he is a man of nature, full disclosure of who he is can result only in restoration of his full human dignity and "honneur" (5) ("honor" [5]).

The Betrayal of Portrayal

In "To the Reader," internal contradictions prefigure the multiple layers of opinion and judgment of Montaigne's *Essais* themselves. These strategies defer closure, in keeping with Montaigne's goal of presenting "some features of my habits and temperament" (611; 3.2). For Montaigne, a man of moderation (146–49; 1.30) who seeks to learn who he is through writing the *Essais*, self-portrayal—like self-knowledge—remains incomplete (611; 3.2).

Rousseau, in opposition, seeks portrayal of the self in "toute sa vérité ("all its truth"). This ambition is what most distinguishes his autobiographical enterprise from Montaigne's. More than Montaigne's propriety, more than his indifference to his reader, more than his humanistic rationale for writing the self, it is the earlier writer's self-revelation that stops short of "all its truth" that provokes Rousseau to challenge Montaigne:

> Je mets Montaigne à la tête de ces faux sincéres qui veulent tromper en disant vrai. Il se montre avec des défauts, mais il ne s'en donne que d'aimables; il n'y a point d'homme qui n'en ait d'odieux. Montaigne se peint ressemblant mais de profil. Qui sait si quelque balafre à la joue ou un œil crevé du coté qu'il nous a caché, n'eut pas totalement changé sa physionomie.   (*Ebauches des* Confessions, *OC* 1: 1149–50)

> I put Montaigne at the head of these false sincere people who want to deceive while speaking truthfully. He shows himself with his flaws, but he gives himself only agreeable ones; there is no man at all who does not have odious ones. Montaigne portrays himself in a good likeness but in profile. Who knows whether some scar on the cheek or an eye put out on the side he hides from us might not totally change his physiognomy.   (5: 586)

Rousseau avoids all mention of Montaigne in the preface to the *Confessions*. Nevertheless, the inescapable conclusion to which we are drawn is that Rousseau had Montaigne very much in mind when composing this preface and that he sought to refute Montaigne's approach to writing the self. And yet, when reflecting on the *Confessions* some years after their completion, Rousseau acknowledged that he had been guilty of the same aesthetics of selection, elimination, and composition of his self-image for which he had so severely taken Montaigne to task: "quelquefois sans y songer par un mouvement involontaire j'ai caché le coté difforme en me peignant de profil" (*Rêv.* 1036) ("without thinking about it and by an involuntary movement, I sometimes hid my deformed side and depicted my good side" [37]).

We can now better assess the boastfulness of the preface to the *Confessions*. What at first contact may have seemed arrogance now appears a mixture of partly justified, partly exaggerated pride at having broken Montaigne's autobiographical mold. What may have struck us on initial reading as overblown rhetoric reveals itself as a troubled expression of Rousseau's insistent need to exculpate himself. In the end, Rousseau's attempt to write differently from Montaigne brought him to the realization that all self-portrayal is to a degree self-betrayal. And it is this anguished awareness of inevitable betrayal that substantiates Rousseau's pretentious—but not absurd—claim to a place apart in the tradition of writing the self.

An Intertextual Approach
to Teaching Rousseau's *Confessions*

Guillemette Johnston

Making Rousseau accessible to first-year students might seem an arduous task, given the difficulties involved in understanding the author's philosophy and idiosyncrasies. Yet students often leave my freshman seminar in English saying they would like to read more of Rousseau.

Each year I hone my strategies to help students deepen their comprehension of the author and his work. Since we are on the quarter system and have limited reading time, I use the *Confessions* as the foundation for my course. This work is ideal for piquing students' interest, and its narrative thread provides continuity. But because Rousseau's life and works so marvelously interpenetrate, much of the quarter is devoted to excerpts from Rousseau's other works that develop, reinforce, and illustrate themes that arise in class. The intertextual approach complements the intratextual approach I use within the *Confessions* and helps students experience Rousseau's system efficiently as I gradually lead them into the problematics of his philosophy and writing. The poetic *Rêveries*, which we read at the end of the quarter, brings closure to the quest for the self, so that students finish the course without feeling frustrated or overwhelmed by Rousseau's complexity. For the sake of brevity, though, I will deal here only with the *Confessions*.

We start by reading books 1 through 3 to familiarize students with Rousseau's formative years. I dedicate the first classes to a thorough analysis of the prologue or preface and the first three paragraphs (3–5 [3–5]). These passages not only introduce Rousseau's intentions but also highlight motifs that surface throughout the *Confessions*, as well as in *Julie* (also known by its subtitle, *La Nouvelle Héloïse*), *Emile*, the second *Discours*, the *Dialogues*, and other works. Taking inspiration from Jean Starobinski's and Jacques Derrida's writings, I create ground rules for reading Rousseau by having students construct grids of similarities and oppositions found in the text. We do not deconstruct the text but simply watch for patterns of sameness and difference. Also, since I like to acquaint students with the less positivist approaches to literature, I try to sensitize the class to disparities between Rousseau's intentions and our responses to him. Students note the melodramatic tone, and their reflection on the rhetoric of the passage helps them identify Rousseau's preoccupation with how he should be read. Rousseau's obsession with readers' reception in the name of justice and true acknowledgment—along with his desire for absolute, innocent communication—draws student attention to the problematics of reading and writing as exemplified by Rousseau's literary endeavors.

The strategy of writing the results of our analyses on the chalkboard reveals how themes reappear in different guises. For instance, displaying the notions of uniqueness and truth and their variations alerts students to Rousseau's fixation on unity and authenticity, as well as his appeal to the natural as the source of both attributes. Our observations on the connection between nature and the true description of man offered in Rousseau's self-portrait raise topics that become central to our discussions of his attitudes toward his work and toward humankind in general—discussions that go on to consider Rousseau's insistence on the opposition of essence and appearance. Close textual analysis also helps students see how themes shift in nuances of interpretation when viewed from the perspectives of the author's intentions, their manner of presentation, and the reader's reception of them. Using our notes on the board as an aid in developing idea clusters, we consider the following questions. How does "la vérité de la nature" (5) ("the truth of nature" [5]) relate to the idea of being knowledgeable: "Je sens mon cœur et je connois les hommes" (5) ("I feel my heart and I know men" [5])? How can one know men if one believes one is different? What is the source of Rousseau's difference? We can then explore such themes as uniqueness, difference, and truth in the context of the themes of accuracy, honesty, frankness, naturalness, sameness, and experience.

We also draw lines on the board to map out contrasts and to look closely at sentences that display obvious yet nuanced oppositions—for example: "J'ai dit le bien et le mal" (5) ("I have told the good and the evil" [5]); or "j'ai pu supposer vrai ce que je savois avoir pu l'être, jamais ce que je savois être faux" (5) ("I may have assumed to be true what I knew might have been so, never what I knew to be false" [5]). As they trace the oppositions of good and evil and of truth and falsehood, students become sensitive to the rhetoric of the text and to the complexity of the passage, as well as to the problem of subjective versus objective knowledge that it presents: Rousseau's difficulties in writing an autobiography that is meant to be sincere and accurate yet must rely on his sometimes faulty memory. From a broader perspective, I encourage students to recognize textual idiosyncrasies by having them identify groups of words associated with similar images, messages, or obsessions. For instance, we isolate expressions with negative connotations—such as "misfortunes," "destroy," "disfigured by my enemies," "cruel injustice," "harmful," "vindicative," "evil," "vengeance," and "contemptible and low"—from words that carry a positive impact, such as "good," "generous," "sublime" (3–5 [3–5]). These interweavings of similarity and difference in the text make students even more aware of the tone, the author's apparent state of mind, and the techniques of inclusion and persuasion Rousseau uses to influence his readers.

The classroom strategy works successfully at several levels—the thematic, the rhetorical, and the psychological—to join concepts across registers and to prepare students for the links between different types of texts that we will make later. As we continue in the *Confessions*, students reflect on intratextual connections by isolating short passages for analysis in relation to themes we have identified. Because students read thirty to fifty pages of the *Confessions* each period and write response essays as well as analyses of selected passages, they gain a deep understanding of the text.

After three weeks we begin alternating our readings from the *Confessions* with weekly readings of passages from Rousseau's other works that develop themes we have been examining: sincerity, authenticity, reading, writing, music, the individual in society, nature, corruption, the plea for sympathy from the reader. We concentrate first on the *Confessions*, highlighting a theme's treatment in different parts of this work, before introducing passages from the other writings. For example, in a well-known incident from the *Confessions*, Rousseau is wrongly accused of breaking a comb at Mme Lambercier's and defends himself out of his sense of dignity and justice (18–20 [16–18]). We compare this passage with the one in the *Confessions* in which Rousseau regrets that he falsely accused a maid of stealing a ribbon that he himself stole (84–87 [70–73]). He traces his failure to admit his crime to his sense of shame, (a result of *amour-propre* triggered by his fear of rejection) and to his exposure to vice early in life, during his apprenticeship (31–35 [26–29]). Once we locate themes such as innocence, pride, and the sense of justice in these passages, we move on to the other works.

Using definitions of key words, such as *amour-propre, amour de soi, pity*, and *perfectibility*, from Dent's or Trousson and Eigeldinger's dictionary, I acquaint students with Rousseau's opposition in the *Dialogues* of *amour de soi* and *amour-propre* (1: 668–72 [1: 8–12]), a crucial element in his belief in humankind's original goodness and *perfectibilité*. We read the preface to the *Discours sur l'origine et les fondements de l'inégalité* (3: 122–27 [3: 12–16]) (the second *Discours*) as well as an important passage on pity (3: 153–57 [3: 36–38]) that students analyze closely, since it not only encapsulates Rousseau's principal ideas on the goodness of humankind and nature and the corrupting effects of reason but also delineates his concept of natural law. Though this passage presents some difficulty, it generates interesting discussions on feeling and thinking and, above all, gives students a glimpse of the foundations of Rousseau's philosophy (pity as a virtue; the role of *amour de soi* and *amour-propre*). Reading this view of Rousseau's theories concerning human goodness prompts students to reflect again on passages from the *Confessions* that we associated with feeling and with a knowledge of human nature.

Next we discuss passages from *Emile* that bring to light what Rousseau calls negative education, a pedagogy that consists in preventing vice from entering the human heart. Indeed, the role of the governor or tutor underlines this technique by making sure that the child remains in a state of *amour de soi* and does not become overwhelmed by *amour-propre*. The passages I select, the garden scene (4: 329–35 [Bloom 97–101]) and the incident of the duck at the fair (437–41 [173–75]), deal specifically with teaching Emile to be humble in handling property and knowledge. These passages, which also illustrate the distinction between acting from *amour-propre* and acting from *amour de soi*, provide a smooth transition for any students who had difficulty with the theoretical presentation in the second *Discours*. Students now see Rousseau's philosophy applied in a concrete manner and can even identify with Emile. After the boy realizes the harm he has done to Robert by destroying his garden, students understand why Rousseau isolates pity as the first natural virtue that establishes order and unity. What sensitizes Emile in this scene and in the scene at the fair is that he undergoes the same ordeal as Robert and experiences the same humiliation as with the "trickster" who manipulates the duck. Through careful monitoring by the child's governor, these experiences make Emile more compassionate. The intellectual journey students take in linking these passages carries them from personal anecdotes (the *Confessions*) to theoretical discussion (the second *Discours*) to a synthesizing explanation that joins theory and personal experience in application (*Emile*). The basic concepts are reinforced in different contexts through repetition.

Other important themes, such as reading, writing, and music, appear early in the *Confessions* and can be found, as well, in passages from *Julie*, the *Dialogues*, and other works, under the rubrics of art, artifice, artificiality, verisimilitude, truthfulness to oneself and to nature, and the variations such themes generate when the writer approaches them from different perspectives. Students can identify the constellation of each theme by comparing Rousseau's treatment of it in several works. Starting with the themes of reading and writing as developed in the *Confessions* and drawing a parallel to *Emile*, the class might move on to the preface to *Julie* (2: 5–6 [6: 3–4]) and letters from this work and end with book 1 of the *Dialogues*. Students can then return to the *Confessions* for a second round, concentrating this time on the role music played in Rousseau's life. They can examine this theme in scenes from *Julie* and, finally, explore it in the *Dialogues*, where reading, writing, and music become interconnected.

Let me offer an example of one of the strains we follow. Early in the *Confessions* (8 [7–8]), Rousseau shows his concern over the loss of innocence that reading can bring about: "je sentis avant de penser" ("I felt before thinking"); "cette dangereuse methode" ("this dangerous method"); "je n'avois rien conçu; j'avois tout senti" ("I had conceived nothing; I had felt everything"); "la raison que je n'avois pas encore" ("my reason which I did not yet have"). These quotations, which highlight the danger of exposing a child to literature too early and thus corrupting his or her direct experience of the world, easily link to passages from *Emile* (only one book, *Robinson Crusoe*, is allowed in the child's curriculum); his education relies mainly on direct experience (4: 454–57 [Bloom 184–86]). Later on, in book 3 of the *Confessions*, Rousseau's account of his character (112–15 [94–97])—and, more precisely, his description of his two sides and of his difficulties in writing—not only underlines his ambivalence toward composition but also prompts students to reflect on their own difficulties in writing. Meanwhile, having students read the preface to *Julie* invites them to consider again the theme of reading and its propensity to corrupt human nature.

Besides bringing up themes already familiar to students, excerpts from the
Dialogues echo the two-sidedness of the *Confessions* as far as Rousseau's description of the fictional character Jean Jaques is concerned. Additionally, parts
of the *Dialogues* offer a sharper view of Rousseau's desire for recognition
while they underscore the paradoxes in his life and career. For example, the
writer's paranoia is marvelously depicted in the long passage (1: 676–90 [1:
14–25]) that begins when the character Rousseau states:

> Il faut avouer que la destinée de cet homme [Jean Jaques] a des sin-
> gularités bien frappantes: sa vie est coupée en deux parties qui semblent
> appartenir à deux individus différens.   (676)

> You must admit that this man's [Jean Jaques's] destiny has some pecu-
> liarities. His life is divided into two parts that seem to belong to two
> different individuals.   (14)

This passage also illustrates the problems stemming from Rousseau's celebrity
as a writer and gives a synoptic description of books such as *Emile* and its
philosophy of negative education:

> il a consacré son plus grand et meilleur ouvrage à montrer comment
> s'introduisent dans notre ame les passions nuisibles, à montrer que la
> bonne éducation doit être purement négative, qu'elle doit consister, non
> à guérir les vices du cœur humain, puisqu'il n'y en a point naturellement,
> mais à les empêcher de naitre.   (1: 687)

> He devoted his greatest and best book to showing how the harmful
> passions enter our souls, how good education must be purely negative,
> that it must consist not in curing the vices of the human heart—for
> there are no such vices naturally—but in preventing them from being
> born.   (1: 23)

Sections on Rousseau's life as a musician as described in the *Confessions*—
including his apprenticeship to M. Le Maître (121–23 [102–03]), his part in
the quarrels over French and Italian opera (382–85 [321–23]), and his work
as a composer (374–76 [314–15])—can be supplemented with Rousseau's
comments in *Julie* on French opera and on Parisian society in general. Letter
23, part 2, to Mme d'Orbe (2: 280–89 [6: 230–36]), parallels and enhances
Rousseau's observations, in the *Confessions*, on opéra bouffe. If time allows,
students can read two other letters from *Julie*. Letter 17, part 2 (2: 245–56
[6: 201–10]), with its acute criticism of French theater (which Rousseau sees
as involving much talk and little action), reiterates passages on the awkward-
ness of the French opera, its lack of simplicity and verisimilitude, and its
tendency to focus on fashion, the grandiose, and the superficial. Letter 14,

part 2 (231–36 [190–94]), which emphasizes Saint-Preux's malaise in society, recalls Rousseau's experience as described in the *Confessions* (115 [96–97]). While treating again the themes of superficiality, the letter brings to light the opposition between essence and appearance. These various themes are echoed, finally, in Rousseau's efforts in the *Dialogues* to establish the authenticity of his musical contributions and his written works (1: 685–90 [1: 21–25]).

Indeed, the passages we focus on from the *Dialogues* project, in a nutshell, the concerns and obsessions expressed earlier by Rousseau—particularly the distinction he makes between *amour-propre* and *amour de soi*. His attempt to defend his character as well as his work and his authorship in the light of his writing, and more specifically in the light of his music, represents a summarizing perspective and underlines the paradox of his wanting to be read at all costs. In an ironic twist, this wish, of course, flies in the face of his arguments on the corrupting effects of reading. Far from bringing closure, the *Dialogues* adds another dimension to Rousseau's work and intensifies the complexity of his career as a writer and of the reception of his writing.

Because the *Confessions* provides students with an accessibe foundation, reading other works does not create confusion but, instead, broadens horizons. Though some of the texts are challenging, detailed analysis of selected passages enables students to master them. Interspersing excerpts and basic texts not only fosters assimilation through repetition but exposes students to works by Rousseau that they might want or need to read later. And because this approach to Rousseau explores many facets of the themes that serve as the backbone of his philosophy and of his works in general, students practice a method of reading that helps them find adequate resources for term papers. For instance, some of my students have been inspired to apply the intertextual technique to the treatment of women in the *Confessions*, *Julie*, and *Emile*. Thus, instead of acquiring an exclusively linear or narrative knowledge of Rousseau and his writings, students reflect on the intricacies of his philosophical system. Gradually they realize that although they have spent a quarter reading one author, there is a great deal more to learn about him if they wish to do so.

Teaching Rousseau's *Confessions* in Translation

Christopher Kelly

Dependence on translations is an inescapable fact of life for anyone who teaches courses on the history of political thought, as I do. An introductory course typically covers authors such as Aristotle, Aquinas, Machiavelli, Hobbes, Locke, Rousseau, and Marx. Reading them in the original language would require a mastery of Greek, Latin, Italian, French, and German, as well as English. Such reliance on translations brings about the curious result that students revolt at reading Hobbes because they have been reading the other authors in contemporary American English and find the English of the seventeenth century too difficult. I once had a colleague who seriously proposed translating Locke's *Second Treatise* into modern American. As strange as this proposal seemed to me, I could not offer a principled objection to it that would not also apply to the translations of the other works in the course.

The one objection that could be raised is that, difficult as it may be for students to read Hobbes's English, the task is not impossible. There are even advantages in the challenge, to the extent that it stems from the changing meanings of words. Hobbes strove for technical precision in his use of certain terms, and his archaic language can force students to follow his diction more closely. In comparison, translations into modern American can be too easy to read because the vocabulary looks so familiar. To give students a sense of the difficulty of the works they are reading, I have always looked for—and on occasion attempted to produce—translations that strive more for precision and faithfulness than readability.

I have found that, despite the problems students have in reading the translation I tend to choose, they share my taste, because they have a rather naive perspective on the faithfulness of translations. A friend in a French department once taught a course on the art of translation, using a text by Rousseau as the original from which his students would work. He told me that one of the students happened to look at a published translation of the original and, from its looseness, concluded that Rousseau had written two different works with the same title. The student had the view that all translators aim at rigorous versions.

My own preferences and practice notwithstanding, I differ from that student in recognizing one argument that leads in a direction very different from the one I take. To some of my friends who teach in French departments, the idea of the introductory course I described above is, at best, amusing. They assert that anyone hoping for an adequate understanding of an author must and will learn the writer's language. Translations cannot reproduce the original, this view goes, and cannot be taken seriously. Therefore, they should be written to provide a pleasurable reading experience rather than to produce a true rendering of the work. In presuming that serious study can begin (although it can never end) with a translation, I am prepared to sacrifice this pleasure. I would like to defend my favorable opinion of translations by addressing two issues: first, the advantages of striving for precision; and second, the usefulness of translations in situating works in an appropriate context.

Certainly the effort to achieve complete faithfulness to the original is as hopeless as it is worthy. While working on a translation of *Rousseau juge de Jean Jaques*, I asked a group of Rousseau scholars how they would translate this title. One suggested *Rousseau on Trial*. The others, more literal minded, saw no difficulty in reproducing the title. Unfortunately, while most were convinced that *juge* was a noun, others (a minority, to be sure) thought it was a verb. This ambiguity cannot be preserved in English, and therefore a more or less arbitrary decision must be made. This problem is discussed, along with references to Rousseau's use of the noun and the verb in the text, in *Collected Writings* (1: xxx).

Sometimes decisions about how to translate a troublesome word or phrase are less arbitrary, and discussing them with the class can serve an educational purpose. One example from the *Confessions* involves Rousseau's use of *patrie*. The term first occurs very early in the work, when Rousseau refers to himself as "fils d'un pere dont l'amour de la patrie étoit la plus forte passion" (9) ("son of a father whose love of the fatherland was his strongest passion" [8]). Forty or fifty years ago, probably only someone who wished to associate Rousseau with fascism would have translated *patrie* as "fatherland"; "country" would have been the preferred rendering. This alternative is appropriate in the *Confessions*, but it would pose a problem for a translator of *Emile* confronted with the remark "qui n'a pas une patrie a du moins un pays" (4: 858) ("he who does not have a fatherland at least has a country" [Bloom 473]). The statement shows clearly what is implicit in all of Rousseau's uses of *patrie*: the term's connotation of membership in a community is much stronger than in corresponding words in ordinary American usage. Asking students to reflect on the difference between "fatherland" and "country" is a useful exercise. Many other terms that challenge translators can be used to raise other important issues. In the *Collected Writings*, Roger D. Masters and I have frequently used notes to discuss vexing terms, and Victor Gourevitch has an excellent discussion of ambiguous words and phrases in his edition of Rousseau's political writings (xliv–liii).

A related issue in the teaching of any book is the relevant context for introducing it. One of the features that make the *Confessions* an excellent work to present is its accessibility. Part 1, in particular, requires little background information to win the interest of students. Many of the well-known people discussed in part 2, however, are unknown to most students today. My experience indicates that even Diderot, Rameau, and Voltaire need some explanation. Nevertheless, I would say that eighteenth-century intellectual life is not the most necessary context into which the *Confessions* can be put. Rather, I emphasize two other contexts, pointed to by Rousseau himself: the tradition of exemplary lives and Rousseau's own writings. Some illustrations indicate the sort of perspective each context gives to a reading of the *Confessions*; the first one shows the virtual inescapability of relying on translations.

In the *Rêveries* Rousseau says, "Dans le petit nombre de Livres que je lis quelquefois encore, Plutarque est celui qui m'attache et me profite le plus. Ce fut la prémiére lecture de mon enfance, ce sera la derniére de ma vieillesse" (1024) ("Of the small number of Books I still occasionally read, Plutarch is the one who grips and benefits me the most. He was the first I read in my childhood, he will be the last I read in my old age" [29]). In his old age, Rousseau read the *Moralia*, but in his youth he read the *Lives* and, in the *Confessions*, he says that "je devenois le personnage dont je lisois la vie" (9) ("I became the character whose life I read" [8]). Rousseau's account of the effect of reading lives is relevant to the understanding of the effect he expects his own life story to have on his readers. Students can experience this effect in Plutarch and compare it with the effect of reading Rousseau. Should they read Plutarch in English, or must they read him in French, as Rousseau did, or perhaps in the original Greek?

A similar question occurs if we consider an even more important element of the tradition of lives. Rousseau does not specifically mention Augustine in the *Confessions*, but he makes numerous references to the author of the rival *Confessions* in the *Lettre à Christophe de Beaumont*, written as he was beginning to work on his own *Confessions* in earnest. Rousseau's silence about Augustine in the *Confessions*, then, can hardly be taken as a sign that he was not thinking about the earlier writer. Thus, the opening statement, "Je forme une entreprise qui n'eut jamais d'éxemple, et dont l'exécution n'aura point d'imitateur" (5) ("I am forming an undertaking which has no precedent, and the execution of which will have no imitator whatsoever" [5]), can be taken as a slap at his most famous predecessor.

There are numerous implicit parallels to Augustine in Rousseau's *Confessions* (see Kelly, *Rousseau's Exemplary Life* 103–07), and they invariably involve sharp disagreements that show why Rousseau refuses to accept Augustine as a genuine forebear. One example suffices. The importance of sinfulness in Augustine's treatment of human nature is indicated by his famous statement "so tiny a child, so great a sinner" (15). Not only does Rousseau insist on attributing his own childhood misdeeds to "bons sentimens mal dirigés" (32) ("good feelings badly directed" [27]) but he does not even use the word "péché"("sin") in his *Confessions*. An adequate understanding of the *Confessions* depends more on an appreciation of Rousseau's presentation of human life—in which sin is not a meaningful idea—than on a knowledge of other writers in eighteenth-century France. In an ideal course on the two *Confessions*, students would read both in the original languages; in a satisfactory class, students can read one or both in translation.

The second context I suggest for teaching the *Confessions* examines the work for the light it can shed on Rousseau's peculiar personality. Frequently, when the *Confessions* is treated in relation to his theoretical writings, it is used to explain, or explain away, aspects of his thought as more or less simple reflections of that personality. Teaching the *Confessions* in political science courses presents the opportunity of reversing this tendency by considering Rousseau's autobiography in the context of his political writings. In the approach I take, I present the *Confessions* as a case study illustrating Rousseau's understanding of human nature. I often teach it together with *Emile*, Rousseau's other major case study meant to illustrate his views on human life.

Emile and the *Confessions* are complementary works in several ways. When Rousseau discusses his choice of an imaginary pupil in the earlier work, he says:

> Quand je pourrois choisir, je ne prendrois qu'un esprit commun tel que je suppose mon élève. On n'a besoin d'élever que les hommes vulgaires; leur éducation doit seule servir d'éxemple à celle de leurs semblables. Les autres s'élèvent malgré qu'on en ait.   (4: 266)

> If I could choose, I would take only a common mind, such as I assume my pupil to be. Only ordinary men need to be raised; their education ought to serve as an example only of that of their kind. The others raise themselves in spite of what one does.   (Bloom 52).

Emile, then, presents the natural education of an ordinary boy. The *Confessions* presents the decidedly unnatural self-education of a man who is not "fait comme aucun de ceux qui existent" (5) ("made like any that exist" [5]). Together these works give Rousseau's account of the ordinary and the extraordinary in human nature, as well as the good and the bad in its nurture.

These general parallels between the two works are carried through in particular details. In both works, thematic attention is paid to the issues of stimulation of the imagination through reading, the awakening of sexual desire, the first experience of anger, and the development of *amour-propre*. To be sure, these themes do not appear in the same order in the two works, and the two move in different directions (Kelly 76–100). Emile is kept from reading until he is fifteen, and his sexual desire, anger, and *amour-propre* are either delayed or repressed. From his earliest youth, Jean-Jacques lives in the imaginary world formed by his reading, and his passions are stimulated in complex ways. These differences, however, are far from contradictory, and the significance of each sequence can be grasped only when the two are compared.

The sort of limbo within which a translation exists is captured by a remark in the introduction to a fine translation of Machiavelli's *Prince*. After explaining the principles guiding his translation, Harvey C. Mansfield says, "If the reader thinks my translation a bad one, let him try his own; if he thinks it good, let him learn Italian" (xxvii). This statement implies, first, that anyone who is a competent judge will find defects in the translation and, second, that anyone who fails to find defects should take the required steps to become a competent judge. Translations are unnecessary for those who know the original language. They can be dangerous for anyone who doesn't, because they may foster the illusion that the reader has understood the work in question when he or she has understood only an imperfect translation. It is easy to reach the conclusion that translations are good neither for those who can do without them nor for those who cannot.

An alternative conclusion does, however, present itself. Translations can be useful for those who are not yet in a position to do without them—for those who do not have the competence to study the original but who might be inspired to acquire it. This description fits most university students, and, in fact, I think that a student might well be defined as someone who is not yet, but might become, capable of pursuing knowledge without the help of teachers or of translators. Adopting theological language, one can say that a translation offers the reflected and dim glimpse of the goal in order to encourage someone who is frightened at entering the purgatory of introductory language study.

"Tout le Monde Se Tut": Problems of Rhetoric in Rousseau's Autobiographical Works

Michael O'Dea

At the beginning of the *Confessions*, Rousseau invites the Supreme Being to gather his fellow human beings around him on the Day of Judgment to hear his story: "qu'ils écoutent mes confessions, qu'ils gémissent de mes indignités, qu'ils rougissent de mes miséres" (5) ("let them listen to my confessions, let them shudder at my unworthiness, let them blush at my woes" [5]). The record of what Rousseau was, did, and thought cannot but provoke a strong response from others, it seems, at least when the presence of God Himself provides a guarantee that the account is true. Within his narrative Rousseau describes moments in which a work of art produces the type of intense emotion that he imagines at the Last Judgment: when Rousseau's short opera, *Le Devin du village*, is performed in his presence at court in Fontainebleau, his audience is ravished by his melodies; similarly, when *La Nouvelle Héloïse* is published, the enthusiasm of his readers gives him deep personal gratification. In both cases, women's reactions are particularly prized (see *Conf.* 545 [456]). At the very start of Rousseau's career as an author, a miniature version of the same success occurs: invited to a noble household in Paris, the watchmaker's son is in difficulty until he saves the situation by reading extracts from his *Epître à Parisot* (289–90 [243–44]).

At the end of the *Confessions*, the reader is confronted by a different and less happy scene. Rousseau has read long sections of the *Confessions* to a distinguished audience. He adds a final declaration, which he transcribes into his text. How does his initial audience react?

> J'achevai ainsi ma lecture et tout le monde se tut. Mad^e d'Egmont fut la seule qui me parut émue; elle tressaillit visiblement; mais elle se remit bien vîte, et garda le silence ainsi que toute la compagnie. Tel fut le fruit que je tirai de cette lecture et de ma déclaration.   (656)

> I completed my reading this way and everyone was silent. Mme d'Egmont was the only one who appeared moved; she visibly trembled, but she very quickly recovered and kept silent as did the whole company. Such was the fruit I drew from this reading and from my declaration.
> (550)

Thus the *Confessions* itself fails to replicate the triumph of previous works. In place of tears and desire, there is only silence, with at most one suppressed response. Although the text recounts some of Rousseau's real successes as a writer, it evokes a positive reaction to the *Confessions* only in a remote, imagined future, and it records the apparent failure, in the immediate past, to obtain any response whatsoever to the work. The significance of this final moment has been heightened just before by an allusion to a possible third part: its absence speaks eloquently of failure and discouragement.

Separated in time of composition by an interval of two years, the two parts of the *Confessions* (books 1–6, books 7–12) do not generally define the reader's relation to the text in the same terms. According to a passage at the end of book 4, the reader can reach a full understanding of Rousseau. The author, it is true, emphasizes his own contribution to the process: if the reader is mistaken, "toute l'erreur sera de son fait" (175) ("all the error will be of his making" [147]). In book 7, the problem of communication has become acute; the final scene with Mme d'Egmont is already foreshadowed. Rousseau's enemies have created major barriers to prevent the truth from escaping. What can he do against such forces? He has "peu d'espoir de succés" (279) ("little hope of success" [235]) even if the project is not abandoned.

After the *Confessions*, when Rousseau takes up his pen again, the motif of surveillance and persecution is again present, but he writes about somebody called "Jean Jaques," in the third person. *Rousseau juge de Jean Jaques*, or the *Dialogues*, is a long meditation on what it is to know another person. "Jean Jaques," it seems at the outset, is a monster yet is allegedly the author of sublimely moral works. Only at the end of a long exchange do the two interlocutors of the *Dialogues* penetrate the calumnies that surround him and arrive at the truth: "Jean Jaques," a good man, is genuinely the author of the works that bear his name. The two decide to end his isolation by offering him their company. So the reader arrives at the kind of happy ending that the

Confessions cannot offer, but by virtue of a complex transposition, for if "Jean Jaques" is offstage, one of the interlocutors in the dialogue is called "Rousseau." By its recourse to dialogue, abandonment of the autobiographical "I," and absence of a narrative structure, the *Dialogues* distances itself significantly from its predecessor.

The third work in the final sequence of writings by Rousseau marks another formal, generic rupture. The *Rêveries* resumes the use of the autobiographical first person but not the narrative form of the *Confessions*. This work will be "un informe journal" (1000) ("a shapeless diary" [7]), and the writer indicates the irrelevance of literary categories by designating each section of the *Rêveries* as a Walk. We see Rousseau shift from the mode of the *Confessions*, with its chronological narrative and cast of hundreds, toward a situation beyond the complex doublings of the *Dialogues*. In this situation, in all simplicity, he is his own reader—"je n'écris mes rêveries que pour moi" (1001) ("I write my reveries only for myself" [8]). On the same page, he also declares, "je ne les cache ni ne les montre" ("I neither hide nor show them"). Other readers are neither encouraged nor rejected, but they are seemingly as irrelevant to this project as they were vital to the *Confessions*.

The changes in rhetoric and in tone that occur as Rousseau's autobiographical works take on their final configuration have often been presented in psychological terms. The *Rêveries*, in particular, has frequently been interpreted as resolving an inner conflict of which the *Dialogues* is the outward manifestation. Thus in an *Histoire de la littérature française* that held sway for some time in French schools, we read: "Despite the tragic pessimism of the work, the *Dialogues* leads Rousseau toward 'his' salvation: the impossible conversation between the three characters is followed by the peaceful monologue of the ten *Rêveries*, composed in the tranquillity of the park at Ermenonville" (Brunel et al. 351; my trans.). (As a point of fact, most of the *Rêveries* was written before Rousseau went to Ermenonville, in May 1778.) Michel Foucault offers a more sustainable version of this argument when, after asserting that Rousseau's previous anguish was prompted by a crisis of language, Foucault describes the sound of lapping waves Rousseau remembers in the Fifth Walk: "in this absolute and original murmuring, all human language recovers its immediate truth and its intimacy" (*Rousseau juge* ix; my trans.).

Taken as a whole, however, the *Rêveries* is not a peaceful work. Such an observation has been made by some of the best readers of Rousseau (e.g., Raymond, *OC* 1: lxxii) and is clearly stated in recent popular editions (Leborgne 33). But observing the terms of the First Walk provides enough evidence: Rousseau has been buried alive by his contemporaries; he is, for them, a monster, a poisoner, an assassin, the horror of the human race. That is the context of all the Walks, including the Fifth, as its first and last paragraphs confirm. (The unfinished Tenth Walk is, arguably, an exception to the pervasive evocation of hostility to the author.) Sometimes, as in the great Eighth and Ninth Walks, misfortune and persecution are everywhere: "La ligue est uni-

verselle, sans exception, sans retour, et je suis sur d'achever mes jours dans
cette affreuse proscription sans jamais en penetrer le mistére" (*Rêv.* 1077)
("The league is universal, without exception, past all hope; and I am sure I
will finish my days in this dreadful rejection without ever penetrating the
mystery of it" [79]). In the more lyrical Seventh Walk, misfortune and suffering
fade into the background, but they retain all their power. Rousseau is "forcé
de m'abstenir de penser, de peur de penser à mes malheurs malgré moi"
(1066) ("forced to abstain from thinking for fear of thinking about my misfortunes in spite of myself" [62]). A series of such constraints ("forcé . . . ,
forcé . . . , forcé . . .") explains his recourse to botany.

Although the *Rêveries* is not a peaceful work, we understand the reasoning
of those who so characterize it. The tone changes, in part, and becomes lyrical
more often than in the *Dialogues*; more intangibly, the reader senses that the
restoration of a single voice, in place of the confusing echo chamber in which
"Rousseau" speaks of "Jean Jaques," marks a return to a happier relation with
language (see the preface in Foucault, *Rousseau juge*). Nevertheless, the thematic opposition between the *Dialogues* and the *Rêveries* is less simple than
is frequently suggested. In particular, the claim, explicit or implicit, that the
Dialogues is the product of paranoia and that the *Rêveries* signals a return to
sanity cannot be defended. If to proclaim belief in an eternal and universal
conspiracy against oneself is to be mad, then the author of the *Rêveries* is
mad, arguably more so than the author of the *Dialogues*, who believed that
after his death the conspiracy would eventually fade away. And if paranoia
characterizes both texts, the differences between them need to be explained
otherwise.

One approach to differentiating between the *Rêveries* and the *Dialogues* is
to organize the reading of the autobiographical works around the inscription
of the reader: even if the result remains hypothetical, the hypothesis has some
explicative power. An important professed motive for writing the *Confessions*,
we know, is that Rousseau was mystified by the persecution directed against
the author of *Emile* and *La Nouvelle Héloïse*. How can the voice of simple
goodness fail to be heard in these works? Can there be any doubt as to the
morality of their author? After Voltaire's revelation that Rousseau abandoned
his children, the recurrent challenges to Rousseau's moral authority have to
be acknowledged and answered. And so begins the vast narrative that will set
the record straight, the portrayal of a man who was sometimes weak but never
vicious, whose actions can always be explained and justified. Because his life
story is inevitably the story of his entanglements with others, he is led to
recount all the mistakes and oddities that prompted hostility, all the moments
when he showed himself "tout autre que je ne suis" (*Conf.* 116) ("completely
different from the way I am" [98]). Soon enough, however, the choice of
writing and hiding described in the same passage reveals its limitations. What
for Rousseau is the evident character of his own goodness fails to compel
assent: there are no tears at the public readings from the work. The author

knows whose fault that must be, as noted earlier: readers or listeners who are mistaken must bear the responsibility. That is so from the beginning, but what in book 4 of the *Confessions* is, at most, a risk becomes, by book 12, a terrible reality. The reader gets it wrong, and the reasons for the error are as evident as the author's own goodness. In the ringing declaration at the end of the work, anyone who studies Rousseau's character and believes him to be dishonorable deserves to be eliminated (656 [550]).

What happens, then, between the *Dialogues* and the *Rêveries* to allow a lyrical voice to be heard more clearly? To answer the question, we have to reexamine Rousseau's own chronology. In the *Rêveries* the time frame is clear, if not always detailed. His present situation, he writes, dates back fifteen years: having at first struggled against his enemies, he realizes the hopelessness of his efforts, resigns himself to his fate, and recovers his tranquillity (995–96 [3–4]). Here, again, an approximate date is possible: his new contentment begins four or five years before he decides to write the *Rêveries* (see the Second Walk, 1003 [11]). Finally, less than two months before the composition of the First Walk, an unspecified event leaves him in a perfect state of calm.

Rousseau's correspondence, however, offers a different picture, inasmuch as themes of resignation and tranquillity emerge far earlier. In a letter to Mme de Verdelin, dated 22 July 1767, he writes, "que les coups de la dure nécessité me frappent à leur aise, je ne daignerai pas sortir de ma place pour leur échaper" (*CC* 33: 229) ("Let the blows of harsh necessity strike me as they will; I will not deign to leave my place to escape them" [my trans.]). A few months later, on 15 December, he explains to Richard Davenport, "La paresse me gagne toujours davantage, la mémoire achéve de m'abandonner. Je jouis des jours qui me restent sans les compter; sans me rappeller celui de la veille et sans projets pour le lendemain" (*CC* 34: 243) ("Laziness is overcoming me more and more; my memory is totally deserting me. I enjoy the days that remain to me without counting them, without recalling the day before and with no plans for the day after"). These statements are in no way exceptional; like the *Rêveries* themselves, the correspondence moves constantly between alarm and resignation. Almost ten years before he begins the *Rêveries*, he often expresses the reasons behind his passion for botany in the same terms as in the first page of the Seventh Walk.

In a short space, it is impossible to give many examples; readers can, however, survey for themselves this mixture of terror and acceptance in the relevant volumes of the *Correspondance complète* (see, in particular, the years 1766 and 1767, vols. 31–34). Even a brief sampling may show that Rousseau's chronology in the *Rêveries* is a rewriting of his own story. Might the chronology be something it does not profess to be—an account, itself rhetorical, of a change in rhetoric? In the *Rêveries*, the external reader is set aside; in the correspondence, Rousseau is writing to friends who are not (yet) suspect: the problem of making the voice of goodness heard and having it recognized recedes, and with it the conviction that his enemies have made his audience deaf to his cries. Now, perhaps, the language of resignation and the celebration of inner resources can recolonize some of the space lost to terror. These are no more than suggestions, but if they are carried further in the teaching of Rousseau's autobiographical writings, the study of shifting rhetorical configurations may yield useful results.

From Reverie to Confession:
Writing and Reading a Life Story

Byron R. Wells

As readers, our students are accustomed to approaching a life story at some beginning point and then proceeding diachronically through its various moments, in order to arrive at an understanding of that life's meaning. While there is no dearth of examples, an obvious illustration is Dickens's *David Copperfield*; the title of its first chapter ("I Am Born") immediately suggests the reading strategy presumed by the text. In an undergraduate humanities course focusing on writings of and about the self, I have found it fruitful to include the *Rêveries*. My choice is based on two fundamental considerations: the relative brevity of the work makes it more accessible than the *Confessions* or the *Dialogues* in a course that surveys European literature; and, unlike most life narratives that we have read or with which students are familiar, it begins at the end of the writer's story.

As useful and even necessary as introductions can be in situating Rousseau historically and in offering generalities about the French Enlightenment, background information on the *Rêveries* should remain brief: students may be more interested in discovering Rousseau for themselves. Their wait is not long. The opening lines of the First Walk invite the reader to ask questions: Who is this solitary narrator? What has he done, or what has been done to him that has led to the social proscription to which he finds himself now subjected? And what does he mean when, at the end of the paragraph, he writes that all that remains for him is to seek what he is (*Rêv.* 995 [3])? To avoid providing what would have to be simplistic answers at this point, and to keep the course as student-oriented as possible, I engage the class in a discussion of the types, causes, and effects of marginalization as a social phenomenon that most students have witnessed and that some have experienced. The discussion should lead to a consideration of the options that remain for the ostracized—indifference, revolt, concession, resignation are the most frequently cited—and their possible consequences. In his own case, Rousseau—as students often observe—suggests the fourth, submission (997 [4]). At this point, they should be referred to the conclusion of the First Walk (1001 [8]), where the solitary walker admits to his authorship of two previous works, the *Confessions* and the *Dialogues*, to which these reveries are avowedly related.

Armed with this new information, students are encouraged to reflect on the significance of the three titles and to infer from them the particular kind of life writing that each might represent. Again, students should call on their personal experiences; with a bit of prodding, they will grasp that the choice of, respectively, the confessional, dialogic, and meditative mode is informed, primarily, by a writer's intended readership and, consequently, by the purpose of the autobiographical enterprise itself—to make oneself known or to know oneself. Because, in the *Rêveries*, Rousseau implies that he is writing only for himself—to seek, in a personal and nonpublic way, what he is—we might understand that his two earlier, public efforts ended, to his mind, in failure. In this light, then, we can consider the text to be the final effort on Rousseau's part to define, even to justify, his life.

During an era in which the marketplace is awash in works of ostensible self-revelation, even the most jaded twenty-year-olds should be struck by one man's multiple efforts to write about his own life, especially one as famous—at least to those who have taken a course in political science—as the author of the *Contrat social*. For instructors, capitalizing on this curiosity is essential, and an effective means of doing so is to follow a reading strategy recommended by Rousseau himself: to proceed through his works in reverse order of publication (*Dialogues* in *OC* 1: 933; *CW* 1: 211). To illustrate the importance Rousseau places elsewhere on this tactic of achieving knowledge, and therefore understanding, of the human subject, teachers can have the class read and analyze both the Second Preface to *Julie* and the preface to the *Discours sur l'origine et les fondements de l'inégalité*. In the first instance, I point specifically to Rousseau's contention that the virtues acquired by the various correspondents can be appreciated only after a long acquaintance with them and their story:

> Mes jeunes gens sont aimables; mais pour les aimer à trente ans, il faut les avoir connus à vingt. Il faut avoir vécu long-temps avec eux pour s'y plaire; et ce n'est qu'après avoir déploré leurs fautes qu'on vient à goûter leurs vertus. (*OC* 2: 18)

> My young people are loveable; but to love them at thirty, you need to have known them at twenty. You need to have lived a long time with them in order to enjoy their company; and it is only after deploring their faults that you are able to appreciate their virtues. (*CW* 6: 12)

In the second instance, the opening paragraph is most telling. Like the statue of Glaucus, human nature has become so deformed through time and events that it is unrecognizable. Yet the situation should not deter us, Rousseau declares, from pursuing self-knowledge and embracing the precept inscribed at the Temple of Delphi (*OC* 3: 122; *CW* 3: 12).

Such readings easily lead to a discussion of the mutability of humankind and, hence, of the sense of self. Unlike the protagonists of works we have read earlier in the course (*Lazarillo de Tormes*, *The Adventures of a Simpleton*, *The Princess of Cleves*) in which the self is represented essentially as stasis, Rousseau posits the self as an entity in perpetual change. When we add to this postulate the obstacles many writers encounter in establishing a language that makes the self transparent not only to others but to the self-seeker as well, the difficulties of the autobiographical project become clear. Though some students may initially prefer (or find it more convenient) to define themselves in terms of a particular constant (e.g., family, acquaintances, religion), a question or two should encourage them to see the self in a state of flux. For example, to what degree have these relationships and understandings evolved since their childhood? Most students will realize that some change in their self-perception has occurred. And if they tried to assess their life story while imagining their own sense of immanence, they would probably be hard-pressed to find the right words. Once students recognize the problems involved in self-expression, they can begin to understand Rousseau's desire to achieve oneness with himself and to discover the truth of his own story by engaging in solitary walks through the past. Alone in the world, with no "prochain, ni semblables, ni fréres" (*Rêv.* 999) ("neighbors, fellow creatures, or brothers" [6]), he is, paradoxically enough, now free to meditate and write without regard for those who have forsaken him and whom he has abandoned.

The *Rêveries*, then, is ostensibly a text whose author declares himself to have no interest in form or readership, "un informe journal" ("a shapeless diary") containing his disparate thoughts about himself and "toutes les idées étrangéres qui [lui] passent par la tête" (1000) ("all the foreign ideas which pass through [his] head" [7]). Students will be quick to grasp the distinction between a work written for oneself and one created with an audience in mind. Many students have kept a diary or journal in which they recorded events of and reflections on their lives. That, in writing the entries, they assumed privacy and were unconcerned that the pages might constitute a diachronic narrative of their lives produced a different kind of text from the one in which the author carries on a dialogue with the self or relates his or her life story to contemporary or future readers. The latter type of writing, be it fiction, documentary, philosophic, or autobiographic, is informed, at least in part, by a desire to persuade readers to accept a point of view. Rousseau, who considered his life and works to be inextricably entwined, was convinced that his critique of Enlightenment objectives (here, some elaboration by the instructor is needed) had led to his purported ostracization.

Whether the alleged plot to discredit him was real or not is inconsequential in this course. My purpose, instead, is to enable students to appreciate the many means by which Rousseau vindicates his life and work against his supposed enemies and to encourage students to reflect on ways this might be achieved. He composed the *Rêveries* following a negative public response to the *Dialogues*, which, in turn, he created after the silent reception of the public reading of the *Confessions*. Although students cannot read the two earlier works in their entirety, the conclusions each work reaches suggest the intention—both present and future—of the author.

In the First Walk of the *Rêveries*, Rousseau the author states clearly that he undertook the writing of the *Dialogues* in the hope that another generation, on reading them, "me verroit enfin tel que je suis" (998) ("would finally see me as I am" [5]); these lines directly echo the final remarks of the character Rousseau in the third *Dialogue*: "L'espoir que sa mémoire soit rétablie un jour dans l'honneur qu'elle mérite . . . est desormais le seul qui peut le flater en ce monde" (*OC* 1: 976) ("The hope that his memory be restored someday to the honor it deserves . . . is henceforth the only hope that can please him in this world" [*CW* 1: 245]). That hope, however, was to be quickly dashed. As Rousseau the author relates in the epilogue to the *Dialogues*, all his efforts to find a sympathetic reader, one who would grasp the truth of his story, were thwarted. The grille before the altar at Notre Dame was locked; the Frenchman and the Englishman to whom he entrusted the manuscript ended their communications with him; even the individuals to whom he tried to distribute his circular letter refused, almost universally, to accept it.

As noted, the *Dialogues* arose from the silent reception given at a public reading of the *Confessions*:

> J'achevai . . . ma lecture et tout le monde se tut. Mad^e d'Egmont fut la seule qui me parut émue; elle tressaillit visiblement; mais elle se remit bien vîte, et garda le silence ainsi que toute la compagnie. Tel fut le fruit que je tirai de cette lecture. . . .   (*Conf.* 656)

> I completed my reading . . . and everyone was silent. Mme d'Egmont was the only one who appeared moved; she visibly trembled; but she quickly recovered and kept silent as did the whole company. Such was the fruit I drew from this reading. . . .   (550)

Rousseau's determination to reveal the truth of the self and to demonstrate, in the face of the accusations made against him, his lack of culpability prompted him to write the *Confessions* and to take up the pen again to compose the *Dialogues*, whose different form—he hoped—would provide a more convincing defense of his innocence. Finding an unreceptive audience in both cases, he withdrew to the solitude of his reveries—where the author, no less intent on being truthful whatever the personal costs, is also his sole and unique reader. Freed from a concern for the opinions of others, Rousseau was now the self-sufficient man whose "shapeless diary" became his final, and perhaps the ultimate, life story, for its self-referential complexity and its ability to engage the interests of readers now far removed from the author in time and space.

The *Rêveries* thus provides students with an excellent opportunity to consider a life synchronically, as a system that is complete within itself at any given moment. The work does not depend on a past to generate meaning, but it invites the reader to move backward in time to uncover the multiple threads that constitute the man and his thought and to see that Rousseau's life and work are irrevocably bound. To illustrate the concept of synchronicity with an example from contemporary culture, instructors can ask students to consider the technique used by Christopher Nolan in his 2000 film *Memento*. Here, the narrative that supplies details about the protagonist's life is developed through a series of flashbacks that constantly return the viewers to the present until they are finally led to the origins of the mystery. Rousseau's text, students will grasp, functions in much the same way, suggesting, as it does, that to engage in the study of human nature entails a quest for origins whose end is self-knowledge.

It is essential to point out that Rousseau writes to be read, whether by others or only by himself. He is convinced of the message he has to relate—of the need to justify and defend his life and to locate an audience who will understand him. As he learned through the various modes he used to convey his story, however, writing a language of the self is a slippery matter at best and one that may indeed be unachievable because of the persistent opacity of language as a means of representation. To demonstrate the point, instructors can ask students to appropriate the three autobiographical forms used by Rousseau (confessional, dialogic, and personal) and to write, with each approach in mind, about an experience in which they were mistreated or unjustly accused (some students may prefer to create fictional characters and events). The activity, which should lead to an awareness of the difficulties in establishing a relation between one's sense of self and a language with which to communicate it, is always enlightening.

The Dangers of Telling It All

Patrick Coleman

In an age of talk-show confessions, "behind the scenes" documentaries, and "tell-all" memoirs, it may be difficult for North American students to appreciate the radical nature of Rousseau's enterprise in his autobiography, or the dilemmas he faced as he tried to explain himself fully to other people—and to himself. Of course, Saint Augustine, in his *Confessions*, had not hesitated to speak frankly of his sins, and Montaigne had readily revealed some less-than-flattering facts about his personal habits—which are sometimes harder to acknowledge than serious sins—but Rousseau faced particular difficulties in attempting to draw a comprehensive self-portrait. These problems stem from the way he brought together, for the first time, two revolutionary ideas about the self. The first idea is the uniqueness of the individual personality, an irreducible sense of self that can be distinguished from all social, cultural, and religious identities and that is experienced most intensely in negative reaction to those external identities. If Rousseau's view is corrrect, then how can this uniqueness be conveyed, without appealing to a vocabulary associated with those identities? In trying to explain how he is different from others, Rousseau might end up merely showing how he is the same.

The second idea crucial to Rousseau's experience is the mobility of the self, a capacity not only to play a wide variety of roles—Rousseau boasts of having lived on every level of French society except the throne—but to identify so passionately and successfully with a new role as to transform oneself, at least for a time, into a different person. In a sense, this ability to assume many identities should bring him closer to his readers, who might find at least part of his life story familiar. But how can the array of personas be made into a coherent whole, except by referring to that unique core behind the parts, and thus undermining the rapport with his readers of which he boasts? Thus, for Rousseau, "telling it all" is more than a matter of exposing the intimate or shameful details that author and reader know must lie beneath the surface of anyone's life. It is also a question of not limiting what he says, because Rousseau *doesn't know* what he needs to reveal in order to make his identity clear enough to be understood and—he hopes—accepted. A major effect of Rousseau's earlier work on the reading public was to upset the conventions about what constituted relevant detail in readers' response to an author. What did Rousseau need to know about his readers to understand where they stood in relation to society as they were now—thanks to Rousseau—beginning to see it? After the catastrophic misunderstanding of his intentions, brought to light by the banning of his books, Rousseau turns this question around and makes it the basis for his autobiography. What does he need to tell his readers to make them understand him?

The answer is "everything." Only by holding nothing back would he prove his sincerity. He would demonstrate his fundamental innocence as well, for a man who dared to reveal everything could not be characterized as bad. Wickedness and dissimulation—from others or from oneself—are inseparable traits for Rousseau. Except in power politics, which operate against a background of violence, Rousseau could not comprehend how anyone could do wrong openly and deliberately. In his own case he believed that the harm he had done resulted from his desire to avoid shame. A prominent example is the story of Marion, the servant girl whom the young Rousseau falsely accused of stealing a ribbon he himself had stolen. Rousseau acknowledges his misdeed in the *Confessions*, but he maintains that his motive was not to escape punishment but to avoid exposure. Only a hardened criminal would actually defy moral laws; Rousseau's lapse stemmed from his inability to sacrifice his reputation—a lesser offense. According to the *Discours sur l'origine et les fondements de l'inégalité* (the second *Discours*), concern for reputation is a bad habit that originated in the move away from the state of nature toward civilization and corruption. Its distorting effect should be resisted. Thus the insidious influence of pride and the desire to please are the inescapable results of socialization. As such, they explain and to some extent excuse Rousseau's failure to be as "transparent" as he would have liked to be. By telling everything—by rejecting the conventions of polite society—Rousseau can compensate for his earlier shameful conformity.

The aspect of the *Confessions* that most dramatically departs from convention in order to tell everything is that of sexuality. Rousseau admits to finding pleasure in the spankings he received as a child, he recalls homosexual propositions made to him as a young man, and he refers repeatedly to practicing masturbation even at times when he was passionately involved with women. Some early readers were shocked by revelations they called "puerile," because these accounts contrasted so strongly with the sophisticated and gallant eroticism of eighteenth-century French discourse. But Rousseau had given up being an "author." Initially, such a stand meant ceasing to write. Now it meant writing but without the work of selection and the respect for decorum that formed the aesthetic and moral basis of authorship in Rousseau's time. To tell everything is to brave embarrassment and shame. It is also to reject the notion of good taste so crucial to neoclassical artistic doctrine.

Of course, the reality of the *Confessions* is more complicated. Rousseau cannot literally tell everything, even if he could remember everything he had felt or done. Some stories will have to stand for others forgotten or set aside, and while Rousseau wants to be frank, he does not want the reader to close the book in disgust. Artlessness only clears the ground for another kind of art. But what kind? According to Rousseau, the familiar paradoxes of polite culture, such as studied carelessness or appropriate sincerity, are almost intolerable compromises. More promising, as a mediating concept, is the capacious idea of nature. On the first page of the book, Rousseau baldly declares, "Je veux montrer à mes semblables un homme dans toute la vérité de la nature; et cet homme, ce sera moi" (5) ("I wish to show my fellows a man in all the truth of nature; and this man will be myself" [5]). By "the truth of nature," Rousseau means that, unlike other self-portraits, which are drawn according to social or cultural convention, his book will convey as directly as possible those feelings and ideas that arise from his particular existence. But "the truth of nature" is not haphazard. In neoclassic aesthetics the term usually refers to a meaningful pattern conveyed through the representation of typical or exemplary features based on the regularity and hierarchy of forms in the productions of nature. Rousseau modifies this traditional point of view by centering both pattern and representation on the structure of the self. While his sexual peculiarities may not conform to common notions of exemplarity, Rousseau believes they form part of a basic disposition toward the world that may sometimes express itself in odd or distorted ways but is "natural" in the normative sense of that word. His character is natural because it is fundamentally good, a term that for Rousseau has a particular meaning. It designates, above all, an absence of those aggressive impulses that disrupt the harmony of things.

Rousseau sees himself as good because his expansive moods constitute a spontaneous embrace of the world as a whole rather than the selection and pursuit of a particular object—operations that involve calculation and the urge to possess. When he retreats into himself, it is not a sign of vanity or resentment but simply a reflection of his wish to enjoy in more intimate fashion his openness to sensation. The autobiography of such a natural character will not hide anything, but it may make mistakes—too much checking would betray an anxiety at odds with innocence. Accepting all the resources of language, it may indulge in what Rousseau calls "ornement indifférent" (5) ("inconsequential ornament" [5]) to supply the gaps in memory or to extend the range of suggestiveness of his discourse. The writer may also leave things out, if they would harm other people or give too favorable a picture of himself. In this way, Rousseau is able to justify some degree of selection and emphasis. As a means of revealing character, "telling all" signifies a quality of intention rather than a quantity of incident.

But the process of writing brings other difficulties to the fore. For example, Rousseau clearly wants to balance what he says about sex with another frank revelation: that in all the intensity of his love for Mme de Warens, he did not desire her physically. He emphasizes the pure, ideal nature of his feeling. But this leads to another source of embarrassment: a man who claimed not to desire an attractive woman who loved and openly desired him cut a poor figure in eighteenth-century French society. In attempting to compensate for the unflattering impression he has given of himself, Rousseau risks reinforcing that impression. One wonders whether his motives are really as selfless as he says. In fact, some of the experiences Rousseau relates, such as the pleasure he took in being spanked, indicate that the revelation of shameful desires is for him a source of masochistic pleasure. But if this is so, then the resolution to tell everything flows not only from a determination to acknowledge his faults, not only from a sense of deeper innocence, but also from another shameful desire: to feel shame itself. Instead of moving from complexity to simplicity, or from confusion to clarity, the act of confession returns Rousseau, and the reader with him, to the problematic mixture of motives the *Confessions* is supposed to untangle.

This dizzying movement of infinite regress characterizes a number of the early episodes, such as that of the stolen ribbon, in which Rousseau tries most directly to distinguish the different levels of feeling and awareness, both in his earlier self and in himself as he is engaged in the process of writing. Rousseau complains that part of his difficulty lies in the vocabulary he inherits from the psychological explorations of the seventeenth-century *moralistes*, adept at uncovering the workings of *amour-propre*, or self-love. Lucid as they were about the duplicity of speech, these earlier writers still held to a generalizing analysis of a static human nature expressed in abstract terms. Rousseau finds these categories misleading because they fail to capture the interpenetration of physical sensation, emotion, and moral awareness in his individual case. Yet, because there is no other vocabulary available, he is forced to use it, and the deeper he digs into any one moment of his past or any one state of his mind, the more he finds himself slipping on the surface.

Consequently, while "telling everything" remains Rousseau's goal, it will not be achieved through any single act of total revelation. By moving away from traditional self-analysis to what he calls the "histoire de mon ame" ("history of my soul") consisting of a "chaîne des sentimens" (278) ("chain of feelings" [234])—that is, the story of their succession, anticipation, and recollection in the course of a particular life—Rousseau will suggest the quality of his personality rather than try to define it as a whole. While the vicious circle of shame and pleasure may never be broken completely, Rousseau can, to some extent, escape its grip by adopting a less strenuous form of presentation. Rather than seek a clear hierarchy of causes and effects in isolated incidents confronted directly, he will follow the vagaries of lived and remembered time, in which moments of varying significance are juxtaposed and their truth glimpsed after the fact, or conveyed between the lines. It will be up to the reader, Rousseau says, to put together what the writer deliberatey reveals and what he betrays unwittingly as he goes along. Rousseau does, in fact, offer an account circumstantial enough to include the gaps, pauses, and jumps that characterize experience as it is actually lived and recalled. In the *Contrat social*, he had counseled his reader to be patient because—although every part of his system was coherent—he could not say everything at once. Here, he expresses confidence that even his own uncertainties and contradictions will help define the fundamental innocence of the man telling the story as best he can. In writing about music, Rousseau had always given priority to the expressive authenticity of melody over the momentary clarity of harmony. Through the unique narrative voice of the *Confessions*, he succeeds in tracing the different rhythms of personal time, the accumulating inner echoes of the past in and behind the present.

The freshness and sense of discovery in the autobiography are achieved at a price. Willing to play with the constraints of logical coherence in portraying himself, Rousseau anxiously insists on imposing an ironclad interpretation on the behavior of other people, whose innocence he frequently questions. Gaps and ambiguities in the stories they tell him stimulate those aggressive responses of reflection, calculation, and comparison Rousseau liked to think were alien to him but which cannot be dismissed. All too often, Rousseau can only turn the complexity of his own feelings into a confirmation of his fundamental innocence by accusing other people of malicious intent. If Rousseau finds his emotions at odds with one another, the cause must lie outside himself, and, since nature (like himself) is blameless, other people must be at fault. Although he makes some effort to control his suspicions, Rousseau repeatedly fails to distinguish between real and imagined slights. He quarrels with his friends because they will not accord him the unconditional love his innocence deserves, and which alone would be proof of their lack of corruption. In the second part of the *Confessions*, he goes beyond the evidence of real hostility to his work—which was substantial enough—and turns mere disagreement or a lukewarm response to his ideas and actions into signs of a conspiracy to do him in. By an interesting paradox, however, the more comprehensive the web of hostility, the more Rousseau is actually reassured, for to the extent that it includes people who have never known or read him, the conspiracy takes on an impersonal quality that allows Rousseau to view it as a phenomenon for which he bears no more responsibility than for a fact of nature. The coherence of the plot makes it an antinarrative, one that lapses into a static and parodic harmony threatening to overwhelm Rousseau's melody but without which, it would seem, melody could not sustain itself.

Untrammeled self-expression and paranoid projection go together in Rousseau. Their connection mirrors in perverse, negative form the fruitful dialectic of self and work that characterized Rousseau's whole career, and especially *Emile* and *La Nouvelle Héloïse*, those books that, before the *Confessions*, were supposed to transform the author's transgressive cultural interventions into proof of his goodness. In a sense, Rousseau had always short-circuited the normal paths of communication in his culture by setting up an alternative and self-sufficient system for defining self and other, personal identity and cultural role, through the writing and reading of his own work. Even more than its content, it was this feature of Rousseau's writing that captured the imagination of thousands of readers alienated in one way or another from the fossilized structures of European society. The problem with Rousseau's autobiography is not, as some critics have charged, that it resorts to artifice but that it is not literary enough. That is, the *Confessions* cannot, except by projecting a conspiracy, create a world sufficiently distinct from that of Rousseau's self to serve as an anchor for their uncertain and anxious author. More than a psychological defense, what we call Rousseau's paranoia is also a desperate attempt to regenerate an unprecedented cultural dynamic, through which Rousseau succeeded for the first time in legitimizing creative writing outside the conventions of genre and the social roles assigned to men of letters. The irony of autobiography, in Rousseau's case, is that it represents both the culmination and the collapse of Rousseau's initial project.

One could say, however, that Rousseau's mistake was to cling, out of pride, to an exaggerated sense of his cultural importance—that is, of his responsibility. Had he been able to give up the burden of representing the truth to and for the world around him, he might have composed a much less strained and disconcerting work, one more in line with the promise of the first six books. Yet even in the darker atmosphere of the second part, lighter passages provide a sudden reprieve from anxious interpretation. The most famous is the account, almost at the end of book 12, of the delightful weeks spent on the Island of Saint-Pierre in Switzerland, just before his departure for England. Because Rousseau's portrayal of the simple enjoyment of the natural setting forms such a happy contrast to the complicated story of real and imagined persecution in the rest of the book, Rousseau may have felt that the account provided the conclusion he wanted and that to act on his plan to write a third part of the *Confessions* would spoil his recovery of a moment of freedom. One can regret the absence of more such moments in the final books of the narrative. In the end, though, what gives the *Confessions* its enduring value is the tenacity with which Rousseau clings to his two contradictory but inseparable goals: to justify himself and his work in the eyes of society and to affirm his own uniqueness—or, rather, to achieve the one through the other. In an extreme form that highlights the pitfalls but also the seductive promise of the genre, Rousseau defined the contours of modern autobiography.

NOTE

A version of this essay appeared as part of the introduction to Jean-Jacques Rousseau, *Confessions*, trans. Angela Scholar, ed. Patrick Coleman, Oxford World's Classics (Oxford: Oxford UP, 2000). By permission of Oxford University Press.

Public Prosecutor Servan
and the Reception of the *Confessions*

Raymond Trousson

Ever since the public readings of the *Confessions* Rousseau gave in 1770–71, many people impatiently awaited its publication. The majority of the curious hoped for sensational revelations about his quarrel with the philosophes. Others doubted the existence of the already famous *Confessions* or thought that the volume would never be published. When the first six books of the work finally appeared, in April 1782, there was disappointment. Instead of the expected scandals, readers found only the account of Rousseau's youthful years and a parade of shameful acts. Old acquaintances, like Mme de Boufflers or Mme Dupin, were said to be disgusted, as were Buffon and Condorcet: the indecency, indeed the disgracefulness, of certain admissions did not correspond to the high esteem in which the author of *La Nouvelle Héloïse* and *Emile* was held. Opinion over the matter immediately became inflamed, as some, like Jean-Pierre Brissot de Warville and Dominique Joseph Garat, admired Rousseau's sincerity without reserve, and others, such as Louis Sébastien Mercier or Jean-François de La Harpe, were indignant about a work that weakened his good name; displayed, in the famous prologue or preface, his unbearable pride; and revealed his obvious madness.

Not long after the reading—which was summarized in newspapers—articles and pamphlets by adversaries and partisans began to multiply. In particular, the *Eclaircissements sur la vie et les écrits de Jean-Jacques Rousseau* (*Clarification of the Life and Writings of Jean-Jacques Rousseau*), which appeared from 1 February to 15 April 1783, in the *Journal encyclopédique*, was published as a brochure in the same year under the title *Réflexions sur les* Confessions *de J.-J. Rousseau* by Michel-Joseph-Antoine Servan (1737–1807). Not an unknown, Servan had been assistant public prosecutor for the parliament of Grenoble from 1757 to 1772. Several works—*Discours sur l'administration de la justice criminelle*; another discourse, *Sur les mœurs* (*On Morals*), and his *Plaidoyer pour la cause d'une femme protestante* (*Defense of the Case of a Protestant Woman*)—had won him the reputation of an accomplished magistrate in the Enlightenment.

While staying in Grenoble in 1768, Rousseau was welcomed by the lawyer Gaspard Bovier, through whom he met Servan. Servan believed he should defend his friend Bovier, whom Rousseau ridicules in the Seventh Walk of the *Rêveries*. Bovier, Rousseau writes, would have allowed him to poison himself by letting him continue to eat berries from a thorny willow. Bovier kept himself from intervening out of a respect for Rousseau that Rousseau treated ironically as "Dauphinois humility" (1072 [67]).

This incident is the point of departure for Servan's close argumentation.

He is determined to warn the public about the "abuse of eminent personalities" and to call into question the responsibility of Rousseau's editors, Du Peyrou and Moultou, for believing that they had the right to publish an account containing an attack on the reputation of an honest citizen. If the reported incident is correct, Servan asserts, the public must henceforth regard Bovier "as either the most stupid or the most wicked of men" (370), as an idiot or as "a cowardly assassin" hiding under a sham naïveté. The danger is not that Rousseau is lying but that the writer whose name can make anyone believe anything might be mistaken in his characteristically vehement affirmations: "What do I want to conclude from all this? That Rousseau has lied in this little anecdote regarding his poisoning? No, but that he himself is horribly deceived" (388). The *Confessions* should therefore be approached prudently, because its author views the world through a distorted lens. Genius does not excuse everything, and the editors should have been prevented from publishing a pernicious text. The Bovier affair proves that it is not the wicked who should tremble but decent men, who can be victimized by Rousseau's twisting of the facts and by his formidable power over public opinion: "To be accused by him is to be already condemned by others, and condemned without any recourse, since conviction comes not from the evidence of the accusation but from confidence in the accuser" (396). Rousseau is "a bilious, touchy, bitter man" who suspects everyone—a portrait adroitly opposed to that of Bovier: "an esteemed citizen, the father of a family," and, above all, an obscure person suddenly disgraced by Rousseau's accusations.

It is not an enviable fate, Servan continues, to be the target of Rousseau's pen, even if Rousseau did not express any previous hostility. The writer has not hesitated to confide secrets that ought to remain unspoken, since they pertain to other persons. Another victim, Mme de Warens, has also been dishonored: "Mme de Warens, whom no one knew, has become famous throughout Europe through Rousseau's *Confessions*. . . . If Mme de Warens were still alive, would these slanders have been printed?" (398). Some people may say that Rousseau compensated for his revelations by addressing to her "the most seducing praises" (399); by speaking highly of her goodness, her generosity: but to what good, since nothing is left to a woman if her honor— that is, her "modesty," the unbreakable natural law—is despoiled. Because of Rousseau, she will remain for posterity merely a creature without morals and without virtue who has been "prostituted coldly and by a pure depravity of principles" (403). Moreover, a moralist like Rousseau has taken it on himself to condemn and not look for excuses. With his talent Rousseau moves his readers, obscures their judgment, leads them in the end "to esteem what he esteems, adore what he adores" (401). What, then, will be said of the woman tempted to depart from the right path? Servan asks ironically from her perspective: "I am quite foolish to resist it so much. What! I resist in order to be esteemed, and here is a woman weak to the point of being a libertine who is nonetheless cherished, praised, respected, and even more by whom? By Rousseau himself" (405). Such a work is disastrous because of the moral authority of its author, who muddles the distinction between what is decent and what is contemptible. The risk is greater than is thought, for Rousseau deceives himself when he imagines that his enterprise will not have imitators:

> Does anyone think that there are not young men to be found who, in the delirium of their *amour-propre*, will not believe themselves to be so many Jean-Jacques, wanting like him to devote themselves to confessions, linking their names to everyone else's, their faults to those of a hundred others, ruining reputations, soiling morals, mingling with and harming their unfortunate neighbors, going about beating their breasts under the pretext of their repentance? If God does not establish order, we will no longer see anything but ingenuous confessions and innocent penitents, ending always by gracefully granting themselves absolution in order better to refuse it to others. (406)

Such a work, which makes public what ought to remain private, should be feared by the social order. Servan condemns not only editors disrespectful of codes of ethics but an author who defames an innocent person and who, by revealing shameful acts that should remain in oblivion, proves the guilty party innocent of these acts—a writer who uses his talent to manipulate opinion and to make one lose the ability to judge correctly.

The *Confessions* therefore does not merit serious attention; the public would be better off if the work was made to disappear, especially since, as Servan concludes (following many others), Rousseau has lost his mind:

> Every attentive reader of these latest writings by Rousseau will be convinced that he has gone mad. . . . I also maintain that by reading Rousseau's *Confessions* with some care, one will clearly see this seed of madness develop from his youth into extravagances, peculiarities, and manias to become a veritable dementia in his last days. (435)

The proofs are not wanting: his calumnies relating to David Hume, his benefactor, whom he accused without any evidence; his obsession with being the object of a universal plot mounted throughout Europe, while in reality he was exposed to less persecution than Voltaire; the outbursts in *Lettres écrites de la montagne*, which have failed to provoke a civil war; his ridiculous tirades against the mistakes of the tanner Thevenin; and the so-called stoning at Môtiers (an argument already used by the adversaries of the Genevan)—a handful of pebbles thrown by "a few naughty Swiss youth" and perhaps no more than a drama staged by Thérèse Levasseur, Rousseau's mistress, in order to get Jean-Jacques to leave Môtiers, where she had grown bored. In short, "the simplest thing, distilled by this ardent mind, could become poison" (388). The prosecutor asks that the consequences be weighed, since the accuser is dead and the offended cannot prove his innocence (396).

In his *Correspondance littéraire* (3: 188), La Harpe fell in with Servan's view without hesitation, agreeing with him that Rousseau's ill-timed confidences were "genuine attacks against the rights of society and the honor of citizens." Julien-Louis Geoffroy expressed a similar opinion in the review *L'Année littéraire*. Unconditional admirers like Brissot, however, spiritedly took up Rousseau's defense. As always, some felt it their duty to stand up for him. Claire Mazarelli, marquise of La Vieuville de Saint-Chamond, with whom Rousseau had refused to start a correspondence, gave a renewed voice to the writer, in her work *Jean-Jacques à M. S°°°*. From beyond this life, Rousseau is allowed to defend himself for having harmed Mme de Warens: she had been corrupted by her first lover, he recalls, and should more reasonably be pitied than blamed: "Do not deny Madame de Warens her good qualities because she had a single vice" (Mazarelli 37). Indeed, instead of an object of indignation, should she not, rather, be "a model to propose to our ladies in Paris" (76)? Subsequently, the lawyer named François Chas brought out *J.-J. Rousseau justifié; ou, Réponse à M. Servan*, in which he says that "all of [the prosecutor's] assertions . . . are false and slanderous" (33) and reminds Servan of the respect due to someone "whom posterity will always regard, despite his errors and his weaknesses, as a friend of virtue and a benefactor of humanity." Also false, Chas asserts, is the claim that Rousseau experienced only imaginary misfortunes: "Show me a single author who received more insults and suffered more humiliations!" (5).

Some observers correctly noted that the *Confessions* would ruin the image of the virtuous Rousseau. Many people were ill at ease when confronted with such revelations, and his adversaries rejoiced to see him condemn himself so completely in the eyes of the public. In a letter dated 9 April 1783, Rousseau's publisher Du Peyrou opened his heart to his colleague Moultou:

> You console me greatly by speaking to me of the success the *Confessions* and J.-J.'s correspondence had with some people. Among men of letters and those who protest their delicate minds and hearts—namely, those charlatans of virtue—there is an unbelievable outburst against the author of these confessions; and the latest example of M. Servan is not proper for making either the first or the true charlatans blush.   (*CC* 45: 137).

The indiscretions regarding Mme de Warens were what particularly upset readers, and, up to the end of the nineteenth century, these passages would continue to be considered scandalous. In 1786, for example, the so-called *Mémoires de Madame de Warens, suivis de ceux de Claude Anet, pour servir d'apologie aux* Confessions *de J. J. Rousseau* appeared. This fabrication was the work of François-Amédée Doppet, an officer of the French guards, originally from Chambéry, who would later be a brigadier general during the Revolution. The preface, which revisited Servan's charges, was harsh toward Rousseau, who is denounced here, too, as "forcené" ("frantic" or "mad"). As for Rousseau's avowals, Doppet contended that they excused nothing: "So much the worse for him, if he believes he no longer has reason to blush from the moment he admitted these things; he must have known that there is a point beyond which a decent man should not go" (iv–v). To Doppet, Rousseau's defamation of the woman who took him in and served as a mother to him is not surprising for this "most ungrateful of men." Doppet then claims that he is publishing Mme de Waren's memoirs, in which she supposedly enumerates the care she took of the young man who placed himself under her protection and who abandoned her without scruple. As we see, Servan's work found a distinct echo and played an important role in the reception of the *Confessions*; his influence would be encountered again and again, whether accepted or contested, even among such admirers as Michel N. Delon and Pierre-Louis Ginguené, or in the first biography of Rousseau, by Antoine de Barruel-Beauvert.

Servan's intentions still need to be examined, however. Cunningly, he presented himself as an admirer of the writer. "Living," as he did, "two hundred leagues from the capital, in deep retirement from the world, as distant from cabals as from the glory that arouses them" (359), the former prosecutor did not want to be the spokesman for any faction. Moreover, he had known Rousseau and could form an opinion of him. Lacking any personal motive, he therefore writes "for the public good" (356), without dreading the sycophants of a writer "not merely famous, but still head of the party" (359). This mask of impartiality explains, in part, the success of the *Réflexions*. Was he not a respected magistrate, accustomed to investigating complex cases, a defender of the law who could not be suspected of bad faith and who, rather than attack Rousseau's person, as Denis Diderot and d'Alembert had done, showed the danger of the *Confessions* for public morals? Servan even conceded that the autobiography contained "a host of admirable things, and some useful ones," but he warned against the excesses of a genius who had lost all sense of proportion: "What is best in civil society is public and private peace. . . . Genius is doubtless a beautiful and grand thing; and fire is also a beautiful and grand phenomenon, admirable when it gives light but ghastly when it causes blazes" (454). And what will happen at the time of publication of the second part of the *Confessions*, in which Rousseau will surely not fail to take on his old friends? Wisdom and civic-mindedness dictate that the editors "officially announce to the public that the sequel to the *Confessions* never existed, or that it has been destroyed" (364), for no one has the right to make of writings not intended for publication "an object of circulation and public discussion"(417). What could be more reasonable than such an argument? If Servan claims to set himself up as an interpreter, it is not of a "sect," as was said at the time, but of so-called public opinion.

The undertaking is not, perhaps, quite as objective as Servan wants it to appear, even if the author maintains, with the authority of someone familiar with trials, that he would "depose" himself "as a witness would be deposed in a judiciary hearing" (374). In fact, Servan had had a burning desire to gain access to the illustrious Citizen and had tried in vain to meet with Rousseau at Môtiers in April 1765 (*CC* 25: 40), three years before chance placed him in Rousseau's presence in Grenoble. But during April 1765, Servan had been better received at Ferney. He had gone there to pay homage to Voltaire, with whom he would correspond from 1766 to 1772 and who wrote to Damilaville on April 8, "He is a good boy and a good recruit" (*Correspondence* 19: 31). For his part, Servan was not sparing in his admiration for the defender of the Calas and Sirven cases. Even if he shared some of Rousseau's political principles, he was assuredly closer to Voltaire than to Rousseau. On 1 January 1768, in a letter to Voltaire, Servan waxed ironic with regard to the *Dictionnaire de musique*, hoping that Rousseau might "be understood more easily through musical rather than political harmony" (Voltaire, *Correspondence* 33: 14). On 6 December 1769, Voltaire praised the *Discours sur les mœurs*, in which the lawyer showed, contrary to the *Lettre à d'Alembert*, that theater can teach good morals. It is not without reason that Chas cast doubt on Servan's impartiality by asking him whether he had ever been "invited by the encyclopedic cohort to write against Rousseau" (4–5). In his *Mémoires*, Brissot de Warville recalls that Servan "was linked with all the philosophes whom Rousseau denounced" (2: 86).

Rousseau had always proclaimed the purity of his intentions, and Servan appears to join him when he concedes that "several of Rousseau's actions accuse him, but almost all of his intentions excuse him" (452). But who knows whether Hell itself is not paved with these good intentions? The task Servan wants to undertake is, therefore, for the public good. Although well-intentioned and sincere, Rousseau is a false sage denounced as the wrecker of overly confident minds and as one whose influence cannot be anything but deleterious. More adroit than Diderot in his brutal assault in the *Vie de Sénèque* or than d'Alembert in the spiteful attacks in his "Eloge de Milord Maréchal," Servan presented himself as a moral authority aloof from intrigues and partisans. He saw it as his duty to warn against an imagined object of persecution, a madman, and a celebrity who manipulates opinion and corrupts minds. His protestations of impartiality, however, hardly cover his ultimately hostile intention.

Translated by John T. Scott

The Author as Celebrity and Outcast: Authorship and Autobiography in Rousseau

Ourida Mostefai

Confessions of a Celebrity

As Rousseau sets out to write his *Confessions*, he is acutely aware of his celebrity status. Indeed, in the first draft of his preface, his public acclaim is presented as the main justification for his autobiographical enterprise: "Si je n'ai pas la célébrité du rang et de la naissance, j'en ai une autre qui est plus à moi et que j'ai mieux achettée; j'ai la célébrité des malheurs" (*Ebauches des Confessions*, *OC* 1: 1151) ("If I do not have the celebrity of rank and birth, I do have another one which is more my own and which I purchased more dearly; I have the celebrity of misfortunes" [*CW* 5: 587]). Anticipating objections to his work, he proudly proclaims his originality: the nature of his fame, which sets him apart from his contemporaries and compensates for his lowly social rank.

This provocative passage bears witness to the profound change in the status of the writer in the Enlightenment. Rousseau's autobiographical writings are the work of a man whose name is known throughout Europe, whose works have been widely disseminated, and whose life has become the object of public scrutiny. Having freed himself from the tutelage of royal power, the author now depends on the public. No longer protected by a system of patronage, he needs to be visible to, and to seek justification from, the public. His works must be circulated and his image promoted; such is the dear price exacted by this new type of celebrity.

As Jean-Claude Bonnet states, the Enlightenment represents the emergence of the public persona of the writer: "Eighteenth-century men of letters are the first to witness both this proliferation of commentary on their persons and the increase in their public image" (262; my trans.). Rousseau's autobiographical writings, then, can be seen both as a manifestation of and a reaction to this new interest in the author as an individual and in the life he lives outside his works.

Rousseau is keenly aware that the public is developing a curiosity about the private lives of authors, that "the image of the man of letters that is gaining ground at the time has a very private character" (Bonnet 261). Voltaire had remarked in his *Lettres philosophiques* that pictures of writers were common in private homes in England. For Voltaire, seeing portraits of Alexander Pope in scores of houses was a testimony to the importance, to the English nation, of men of letters—a proof of their public recognition. Half a century later, Rousseau would experience the burgeoning of the personal cult of the author, complete with visits, fan mail, and pilgrimages. Thus in insisting, as he does, on "telling it all," Rousseau is responding to and exploiting the public desire to peer into an author's private life.

The *Confessions* and the *Rêveries* are thus a response to this inquisitiveness, to this eagerness for knowledge of the person behind the writing. According to Rousseau, his publisher Marc-Michel Rey had urged him to write his memoirs. But in choosing to offer his *Confessions*, Rousseau moves beyond the boundaries of the more established genre and proposes to satisfy the public's demand for information by providing previously unpublicized self-explanations and other personal subjects. What motivates Rousseau is the wish not merely to publish his story but to alter his public perception—to correct the distorted picture that his enemies have circulated about him. The *Confessions* is Rousseau's attempt to reshape the reception of his work that has been based on a misrepresentation of its author. Addressed to the public—both present and future—the *Confessions* thus seeks to substitute one image of the celebrated author for another: "Il y avoit un Rousseau dans le grand monde, et un autre dans la retraite qui ne lui ressembloit en rien" (*Ebauches* 1151) ("There was a Rousseau in high society, and another in retirement who bore no resemblance to him" [587]). Rousseau draws a sharp contrast between the falsity of the public image and the truth of the private one. Writing about himself will allow him to undo the damage caused by fame; for fame has produced a distorted image, a lie that conceals the author's true self.

For Rousseau, the autobiographical task necessarily involves the reeducation of a public that must be consistently informed and corrected in its views so as to be able to make a thoughtful choice. Even the *Rêveries*, which Rousseau claims to be writing only for himself, continues the process of correction. In the later text, he tries to "set the record straight" by offering minute details of actual events. In the Second Walk, for instance, the reader is presented with an account of the Ménilmontant accident that closes with the following statement, in the fashion of a bureaucratic (police) document: "Voila très fidellement l'histoire de mon accident" (1006) ("That, very faithfully, is the story of my accident" [13]).

The *Dialogues* carries this instructional enterprise one step further by presenting the two identities of the author jointly (that of Rousseau, and that of Jean-Jacques) and helping the reader differentiate between the private self and the public image. By including embarrassing revelations, Rousseau displays a side of himself not yet known by the public and, at the same time, responds to his accusers. The "private" facts revealed in the *Confessions* are supposed to counteract the falsehoods of the *Sentiments des citoyens*, the anonymous pamphlet now believed to have been written by Voltaire and in which Rousseau was accused of having abandoned his children to the streets. The accusation regarding their abandonment needs to be clarified and the misleading statements in the character assassination revealed. By admitting his guilt, Rousseau nevertheless insists on his innocence: he has abandoned his children, but he has not harmed them, as the *Sentiments du citoyen* had claimed.

For the question is: Who has the right to judge the author? Rousseau systematically claims that the public is the only legitimate judge. Interestingly, by setting up a sharp division between the public opinion on his side and the world of letters against him, Rousseau makes his celebrity status rest on his popularity among readers. He becomes a creation of the public, a popular writer despised by the literary establishment. This is not a pure invention, of course, since we know that the reception of many of Rousseau's works followed such a pattern. For instance, according to Louis Sébastien Mercier, the reception of *Julie* was characterized by a rift between the general public and the literary elite: "Writers rejected the effect of the work as much as they could; the public took it up in good faith" (qtd. in Trousson, *Mémoire de la critique* 535; my trans.). Indeed, as Maurice Cranston points out, the popular response "transformed the author from a literary celebrity into a cult figure" (*Solitary Self* xi).

Celebrity and Outcast

We see now the paradoxical character of Rousseau as a literary figure: he is simultaneously famous and marginal. One of the most acclaimed men of the Enlightenment is also, by his own account, the most obscure: "Parmi mes contemporains, il est peu d'hommes dont le nom soit plus connu dans l'Europe et dont l'individu soit plus ignoré" (*Ebauches* 1151) ("Among my contemporaries there are few men whose names are more known in Europe and whose person is more unknown" [587]).

If we are to believe him, Rousseau's career lasted about ten years, from the publication of his first *Discours* (*Discours sur les sciences et les arts*) to the publication of *Emile* and the *Contrat social*. Throughout his work and his correspondence, when Rousseau recounts his entry into the world of letters, he insists that his debut was never an act of will. Repeatedly, he describes this episode as having occurred "in spite of himself," against his will, as well as against all odds.

In a letter written in 1735, in response to his father's questions regarding his future, Jean-Jacques considers three possible careers: musician, secretary, and preceptor (tutor). They are, we might note, three professions that Rousseau will actually hold: as composer of *Le Devin du village*, secretary to the French ambassador in Venice, and preceptor of the Mably children. For the young Rousseau, being a man of letters is neither a profession nor an established position. He continually insists on his lack of vocation for writing, on the difficulty and the suffering he must endure in his work: "On s'imaginoit que je pouvois écrire par métier comme tous les autres gens de lettres, au lieu que je ne sus jamais écrire que par passion" (*Conf.* 513) ("They imagined that I could write as a trade as all the other literary people did, instead of which I could never write except out of passion" [430]).

In the *Confessions*, Rousseau states that "depuis quelque tems, je formois le projet de quitter tout à fait la litterature et surtout le métier d'Auteur" (514) ("For some time, I had been forming the plan of leaving literature altogether and above all the trade of Author" [430]). One of the leitmotifs of the autobiographical texts is his claim to have abandoned the literary career: "Ayant quitté tout à fait la litterature, je ne songeai plus qu'à mener une vie tranquille et douce autant qu'il dépendroit de moi" (601) ("Since I had given up literature completely, I no longer thought of anything but leading a tranquil and sweet life as far as it depended on me" [503]). Rousseau seems simultaneously to be giving up on the status of man of letters and claiming to reinvent it, of finding a new language for it.

Rousseau had begun his career with an accusation against his contemporaries, guilty according to him of having been seduced and corrupted by a pseudophilosophy. This accusation is meant to be both general and particular: directed at society as a whole for having substituted the appearance of virtue for real virtue, but also specifically at the society of men of letters: "cette foule d'Ecrivains obscurs et de Lettrés oisifs, qui dévorent en pure perte la substance de l'Etat" (first *Discours*, OC 3: 19) ("that crowd of obscure Writers and idle men of Letters who uselessly consume the substance of the State" [CW 2: 19]). The personal transformation he recounts in his autobiographical writings is offered to the readers as a testimony to his fundamental difference from the literary establishment, a difference based on his sincerity.

Readers of Rousseau's autobiographical writings are confronted with two seemingly incompatible images of the author. On the one hand, Rousseau presents himself as a celebrity whose name is known throughout Europe and who laments the loss of privacy that results from fame. On the other hand, Jean-Jacques is portrayed as an outcast, banished from his contemporaries, and condemned by a vast conspiracy to solitude and marginality:

> Me voici donc seul sur la terre, n'ayant plus de frere, de prochain, d'ami, de societé que moi-même. Le plus sociable et le plus aimant des humains en a été proscrit par un accord unanime. (*Rêv.* 995)

> I am now alone on earth, no longer having any brother, neighbor, friend, or society other than myself. The most sociable and the most loving of humans has been proscribed from society by a unanimous agreement. (3)

It is the strategy of the *Confessions* and the *Rêveries* to portray Rousseau in a state of solitude. However, the reading of the correspondence can help us correct this impression. Indeed, what the letters reveal is that, in exile, Rousseau continues to be a celebrity: streams of visitors come to visit him, seeking advice or simply wanting to meet the great man. Furthermore, as Frédéric Eigeldinger's research has shown (167–73), while in exile in Môtiers, Rousseau carefully cultivated an image of himself as a solitary figure, artfully concealing from his visitors his very real engagement in contemporary controversies and disputes. Rousseau's exile did not simply contribute to his fame; it was enlisted in the author's effort to construct and reconstruct his famous persona.

We know that Marie Antoinette paid homage to Rousseau's tomb on the Ile des peupliers. Could it be that Marie Antoinette found, in Rousseau's fate, solace for her own difficult fame? Perhaps. She would certainly not be the last of the celebrities and outcasts to identify with the "misfortune" of Jean-Jacques.

CLOSE READINGS

Truth and the Other in Rousseau's *Confessions*

Christie McDonald

Teaching Rousseau's *Confessions* at the beginning of the twenty-first century, with renewed interest in ethics and popular forms of personal and testimonial writing, presents certain philosophical and formal challenges. Rousseau writes his life story as both a philosophical model for understanding humanity and a unique mission: "Je sens mon cœur et je connois les hommes" (5) ("I feel my heart and I know men" [5]). The task is to situate this writing about life in the broader context of Rousseau's social and political work. By reading the comb scene, in book 1 of the *Confessions*, in relation to the early anthropological works and a series of sketches for the *Confessions*, instructors can show how truth emerges not only as a pact between author and reader, as Philippe Lejeune has suggested for all autobiography, but as a social contract (however inadequately realized) between self and other. The need for the contract is born out of the rough transition from a utopian vision of a natural state to the facts of history and culture, in which a bond is created that is the necessary result, beyond anarchy or revolution, of Rousseau's primary intuition about the discontinuity between the two.

Rousseau came to these first principles only in his autobiographical writing. His work divides into three major periods: the early anthropological writings (the first and second *Discours* and the *Essai sur l'origine des langues*); the great sociopolitical books written in the 1750s and early 1760s (*Emile*, *La Nouvelle Héloïse*, and the *Contrat social*); and the late autobiographical writings (the *Confessions*, along with the *Dialogues* and the *Rêveries*). Instructors might teach all the books separately, in the context of various courses, but I prefer to teach the autobiography, when possible, in conjunction with the earlier work.

In the *Discours sur l'origine et les fondements de l'inégalité* (second *Discours*), Rousseau describes a hypothetical history of humankind in which he largely throws out the facts, then establishes a trajectory leading from the state of nature to a morally degenerate social order. Because of historical change, he argues, observation of contemporary society cannot result in an understanding of the true nature of humanity. Before discussing natural law, Rousseau sets forth two principles essential to humanity's "natural morality": love of oneself as survival instinct and pity as commiseration with others. Pity is the compassionate sentiment from which love and all other social relations derive. The debate around the status of pity and its development in Rousseau's concept of the state of nature merits examination: Can sociability and the potential for human progress conceivably be inherent in a state described as pure and ahistorical? Or does pity evolve when social relations arise and the faculty of the imagination allows for a conception of the other (see Derrida; de Man; and Starobinski, *Transparency*)?

The view of early society as pacific rather than violent, and as the project of social renewal, necessitates a concept of the passage from the state of nature and the onset of society. In the anthropological works, Rousseau provides a mythic account of societies born from natural catastrophes; in the sociopolitical writings, renewal of the social order comes about through pedagogy (*Emile*), a story of passion and family (*Nouvelle Héloïse*), and finally a social contract (*Contrat social*); in the autobiography, Rousseau explains how he differs from his contemporaries and recovers a complex inner being that is equivalent to the natural state of human beings. If what distinguishes humankind from animals is perfectibility and the consciousness of liberty—both conditions of progress—therein lies, as well, the road to moral disintegration. So Rousseau narrates in the autobiography the story of an individual caught between the threat of present-day moral turpitude and an innate yearning for a purer and better world.

The *Confessions* is often considered to be the first modern autobiography, a claim Rousseau took one step further: "Je forme une entreprise qui n'eut jamais d'éxemple, et dont l'exécution n'aura point d'imitateur. Je veux montrer à mes semblables un homme dans toute la vérité de la nature; et cet homme, ce sera moi" (5) ("I am forming an undertaking which has no precedent, and the execution of which will have no imitator whatsoever. I wish to show my fellows a man in all the truth of nature; and this man will be myself" [5]). Still, pointing to Saint Augustine in the Christian tradition while scolding Montaigne's "partial" secularized portraits in essay form, Rousseau sets an altered course. He writes about his own life as both singular and contingent but at the same time universal in his bond with the truth of humankind.

Rousseau appeals in his argument to readers' sensibility rather than to their rational capacity:

Qui que vous soyez que ma destinée ou ma confiance ont fait l'arbitre du sort de ce cahier, je vous conjure par mes malheurs, par vos entrailles, et au nom de toute l'espéce humaine de ne pas anéantir un ouvrage unique et utile, lequel peut servir de prémiére piéce de comparaison pour l'étude des hommes.   (3)

Whoever you may be whom my destiny or my trust has made the arbiter of the fate of this notebook, I entreat you by my misfortunes, by your innermost emotions, and in the name of the whole human species not to destroy a unique and useful work which can serve as the first piece of comparison for the study of man.   (3)

Because feeling defines existence in his view, Rousseau relies on comparison and the reinforcement of subjective experience by the example of another. In the sketches for the *Confessions*, meditating on how best to prove the truth of the self, he lays out a strategy in a series of fragments (*OC* 1: 1148–72). Here is the gist of the passages. The first requirement is to know another in order to situate the self in the "ordre moral": "Il faudroit connoitre outre soi du moins un de ses semblables, afin de démeler dans son propre cœur ce qui est de l'espéce et ce qui est de l'individu" (*Ebauches des* Confessions [ms. from N, fragment 3], in 1: 1158) ("Besides oneself, it is necessary to know at least one fellow creature in order to distinguish what in one's heart belongs to the species and what to the individual") (my trans.). Many people wrongly believe they know others, as the erroneous judgments of Rousseau by contemporaries attest. Without an interior model to pass from the individual to transcendent truth provided in Augustine's autobiography, the secular self seems condemned to false sincerity or mistaken (not to say malevolent) judgment. Rousseau touches here on the relation between biography and autobiography, relating the two in a complex choreography. If one is able to judge others by oneself, then proof comes with the rule that it is necessary to know at least one other to avoid error. And this conclusion leads Rousseau to his skillful defense of confessional truth, demonstrated in the following series of fragments:

> Je veux tacher de faire qu'on puisse avoir du moins une piéce de comparaison, que chacun puisse connoitre soi et un autre et cet autre ce sera moi.
>
> (*Ebauches des* Confessions [ms. from N, fragment 4], in 1: 1158)
>
> I would like to see to it that there be at least one comparison piece: each person can know himself and another, and this other will be myself.
>
> (my trans.)

J'écris la vie d'un homme qui n'est plus, mais que j'ai bien connu, qu'ame vivante n'a connu que moi et qui merita de l'être. Cet homme c'est moi même. Lecteurs, lisez attentivement cet ouvrage; car bien ou mal fait il est unique en son espéce.

(*Ebauches des* Confessions [ms. from N, fragment 5], in 1: 1159)

I am writing the life of a man who is no longer, someone known to no other living soul but myself and who was worth knowing. This man is myself. Readers, read this work carefully, for whether it is well or badly done, it is one of a kind.

While solitude and difference distinguish Rousseau from his contemporaries, they do not complete the test of veracity. He must bring the qualities of feeling and sensibility into social relationships based on a universal "sensitive" cogito with the principle of pity: "Moi seul. Je sens mon cœur et je connois les hommes" ("Myself alone. I feel my heart and I know men.") The disclosure of "secret causes" in the relation between the private and the public is what Malraux, among others, later rejected in Rousseau's work: not only personal revelation but the humiliating exhibition of human weakness, which did not seem fitting to the public engagement of the intellectual. Yet Rousseau's goal was to create a space for the inner self (the infallible "conscience") to reflect on life's failings as well as its triumphs, a space coextensive with the social and political sphere.

In book 1 of the *Confessions*, Rousseau recounts how he passes through stages similar to those, described in the second *Discours*, of the hypothetical history of humankind; he recalls how his blissful life in the country home of the Lambercier family at Bossey comes abruptly to an end with the first encounter of social injustice. He is wrongly accused by circumstantial evidence of breaking the teeth of a comb left out to dry. Recounting the scene decades later, at age fifty, the autobiographer defends his innocence and expresses himself with a sense of moral outrage as strong as it had been at the time. He not only links childhood to adulthood, and sensibility to reflection, but provides the subsequent connection from self to other: with time, he transfers the feelings associated with this event to the lives and actions of others:

et ce sentiment, relatif à moi dans son origine, a pris une telle consistance en lui-même, et s'est tellement détaché de tout interest personnel, que mon cœur s'enflamme au spectacle ou au récit de toute action injuste, quel qu'en soit l'objet et en quelque lieu qu'elle se commette, *comme si l'effet en retomboit sur moi* [emphasis added]. Quand je lis les cruautés d'un tyran féroce, les subtiles noirceurs d'un fourbe de prêtre, je partirois volontiers pour aller poignarder ces misérables, dussai-je cent fois y périr. Je me suis souvent mis en nage, à poursuivre à la course ou à coups de pierre un coq, une vache, un chien, un animal que j'en voyois tourmenter un autre, uniquement parce qu'il se sentoit le plus fort. (20)

and this feeling [of violence and injustice], relating to myself in its origin, has taken such a consistency in itself, and has been so much detached from all personal interest, that my heart is inflamed at the spectacle or narrative of all unjust actions—whatever their object might be and wherever they are committed—*just as if their effect fell on me* [emphasis added]. When I read the cruelties of a ferocious tyrant, the crafty foul deeds of a cheat of a priest, I would willing[ly] set off in order to stab those wretches, even if I were obliged to perish a hundred times in doing so. I have often gotten myself bathed in perspiration, by pursuing at a run or by throwing stones at a rooster, a cow, a dog, an animal that I saw tormenting another one, solely because it felt itself to be stronger. (17)

Here ends the serenity of a childhood that had reproduced the Judeo-Christian schema: "Nous restames encore à Bossey quelque mois. Nous y fumes comme on nous réprésente le prémier homme encore dans le paradis terrestre, mais ayant cessé d'en joüir" (20) ("We remained at Bossey for several months. We were there as the first man is represented to us in the terrestrial paradise, but we had ceased to enjoy it" [18]).

As the child leaves his paradise, the writer, in a reversal of images, exchanges the theological model for a secular testimonial to an emerging social conscience. The comb used for enhancing one's looks has preempted the symbolic apple, which appears a few pages later in parodic repetition of Augustine's pear-stealing scene (in book 8 of his *Confessions*) and is designed to show that fruit is not the object but that evil itself is. And in the third *Dialogue*, interlocutor Rousseau turns the unreliability of images against his presumed enemies:

Supposez qu'un homme vous dise: J.J. dit qu'on lui a volé des poires, et il ment; car il a son compte de pommes; donc on ne lui a point volé de poires: ils ont exactement raisonné comme cet homme-là, et c'est sur ce raisonnement qu'ils ont persifflé sa déclaration.   (*OC* 1: 960)

Suppose that a man says to you: J.J. says some pears have been stolen from him and he is lying, because he has all his apples, so nobody stole any pears from him. They reasoned exactly like that man, and using this reasoning they ridiculed his declaration.   (*CW* 1: 233)

In the slippage from apples to pears to a comb, in the fall from innocence, Rousseau has vindicated himself and others from original sin: the fall from nature being an act beyond humankind's will. His subsequent participation in all manner of mischief, in a postlapsarian society, repeats the pattern of moral breakdown established in the anthropology.

The comb scene underscores two aspects of Rousseau's thought: first, the end of a natural ethics of sympathy and care in the history of the individual and society; second, the need to find another self (his cousin as double, himself in the past) to explain the need for radical change in a degenerate world. The lesson of social injustice is that, once the break between nature and culture has occurred, human beings must establish conventions, law, and a social contract. But because the facts of history have discredited the ideal, Rousseau formulates the concept of mutual obligation in the *Contrat social* apart from action and change. Having envisaged the *Confessions* in three parts, Rousseau ends the second with a disastrous public reading and never writes the third. Rather, he composes the *Dialogues*, in which an imagined Frenchman attacks the character J.J. and allows his other self, Rousseau, to defend the relation between life and work. The lesson of the comb scene, like that of the gloomy perception of relations with Rousseau's contemporaries, is that reconstruction of society must take place outside time and history, through a pact that opposes the general to the particular will. In the newly imagined society, pity, the faculty for connection with another, will link the self with all others in an undivided social bond.

Rousseau's Lottery

Thomas M. Kavanagh

Rousseau's notes for the *Rêveries* have come down to us in a surprising form. At the Bibliothèque de Neuchâtel there are twenty-seven playing cards whose backs, as was the practice in the eighteenth century, were printed as plain white sheets, something like an unlined index card. On each of the backs there are, in Rousseau's hand, disjointed paragraphs of a few sentences. Most are in pencil, and some were later traced over in ink. Rousseau probably put a few playing cards in his pocket when he set off on his afternoon walks in the countryside around Paris. Should a thought occur to him that would be useful for the *Rêveries*, which he spent his mornings composing, he would jot it down on the back of a playing card. On one level, it seems incongruous that Rousseau, who roundly condemned all forms of gambling as a Parisian perversion, should have a supply of playing cards so close at hand. On another level, playing cards as emblems of random chance seem well suited to what Rousseau saw as distinctive about the *Rêveries*. In the First Walk he announces his intention: "Je dirai ce que j'ai pensé tout comme il m'est venu et avec aussi peu de liaison que les idées de la veille en ont d'ordinaire avec celles du lendemain" (1000) ("I will say what I have thought just as it came to me and with as little connection as the ideas of the day before ordinarily have with those of the following day" [7]).

Capturing the random meanderings of consciousness is not something we usually associate with Rousseau. His defining concern had been with elaborating narratives so compelling in their arguments that their truth could not be resisted. His primarily narrative ambition took two forms, political theory and autobiography. The two *Discours* and the *Contrat social* strive to reveal within their narratives the hidden truth of humankind's lost past, tragic present, and possible future. The *Confessions* and *Dialogues* offer narratives of a life and a martyrdom that demonstrate their author's unique innocence. Rousseau the historian of a universal degradation within society would, after his death, be championed by the Revolution as the sage who broke the chains of oppression and earned a place of privilege in the modern Pantheon.

Narrative does not actually disappear in the *Rêveries*; rather, the continuity it would establish between past, present, and future becomes a tribute of suffering paid to hostile others. Writing only for himself, renouncing all hope that his words might convince or even reach anyone else, Rousseau turns away from the carefully articulated cogencies of narrative. The new form of writing, divided into "Walks," will have as its only goal the preservation of the moment's ecstasy, of those rare instances in which Rousseau can escape the vicious narratives of his life circulated by his enemies. The dynamic driving the *Rêveries* is the tension between the inscription of epiphanic moments and a lingering need to respond to the lies he sees substituted for his truth. Time and again, as the menacing falsehoods of others reassert themselves, Rousseau yields to the narrative temptation. Each time the compulsion to tell his story takes over, Rousseau's only relief from paranoia is to end his Walk and stop writing, hoping to begin anew under the inspiration of some future privileged moment.

The contradictory impulses at work here are particularly apparent in the Ninth Walk. A text with two beginnings, it starts first as a page-long amplification of a sentence jotted down on one of the playing cards: "Le bonheur est un etat trop constant et l'homme un être trop muable pour que l'un convienne à l'autre" (1166) ("Happiness is a state too constant and man a being too changing for the one to suit the other" [my trans.]). That thought becomes, in the Ninth Walk, a sustained contrast between two distinct forms of well-being. On the one hand, there is the pure moment of a "contentment" ("contentment") born within the "flux continuel" ("constant flux") of experience and alien to any "projets pour l'enchainer" ("plans to chain it up"). On the other hand, there is "happiness" with the continuity of "un état permanent qui ne semble pas fait ici bas pour l'homme" (1085) ("a permanent condition which does not seem to be made for man here-below" [78]). Earlier, in the Fifth Walk, Rousseau struggled with the same paradox in describing the felicity he discovered during his six-week stay on the Island of Saint-Pierre. There he juxtaposes the "courts momens de délire" ("short moments of delirium") brought by "du plaisir qui passe" ("transitory pleasure") with a "bonheur qui dure" ("happiness which lasts"), adding immediately that "je doute qu'il y soit connu" ("I doubt that it is known here"). Contentment and delirium may never achieve the hallmark continuity of happiness, because they occur within a present surrounded by a past "qui nous fait regreter quelque chose avant" ("which makes us long for something beforehand") and by a future that makes us "desirer quelque chose après" (1046) ("desire something else afterward" [45–46]).

The solution to this dilemma—the solution that generates the *Rêveries* as a text—is to use the atemporal present of writing (and eventual rereading) to re-create in words a remembered *délice* that is freed from the threats of past and future. As part of a lived present, that privileged moment can exist only as a contentment doomed to disappear. Reborn within writing, it can achieve the durability of true happiness.

As conceptually satisfying as this Proustian solution might be, it fails Rousseau on two counts. No matter how consoling that scriptural euphoria might be, the degraded present of a world shaped by the hostility of others continually intrudes upon his consciousness. The remembering and writing self cannot maintain its isolation, oblivious to a world molded by sinister designs. At the same time, the solipsistic ideal of a self concerned only with reliving its past flies directly in the face of what Rousseau saw as an essential component of authentic happiness: that it be shared with those around him. For this reason the prologue to the Ninth Walk ends with an unanswerable question:

"Est-il une jouissance plus douce que de voir un peuple entier se livrer à la joye . . . et tous les cœurs s'épanouir aux rayons suprêmes du plaisir?" (1085) ("Is there a sweeter enjoyment than to see a whole people give itself up to joy . . . and every heart expand in the broad rays of pleasure?" [78]).

When Rousseau returns to his text, we realize why this first start aborted so quickly. Beginning again, he mentions that, three days earlier, a friend brought him, "avec un empressement extraordinaire" ("with extraordinary haste"), a copy of the eulogy d'Alembert had just published of the recently deceased Mme Geoffrin. In that short work, d'Alembert praises Geoffrin's devotion to the welfare of children and her concern that all prospective spouses be certain that they are ready to assure their children the love and care they need. D'Alembert quotes her as frequently asking engaged couples, "Que deviendront vos pauvres enfans, s'ils vous perdent de bonne heure?" ("Eloge de Mme Geoffrin," qtd. in *OC* 1: 1824n5) ("What will become of your poor children, if they lose you too soon" [*CW* 8: 295n4]). For Rousseau, that question brings up the painful subject of his own rejection of fatherhood, of his having handed over to a foundling home all five of the children he had with Thérèse. Once recovered from what he saw as a direct accusation of himself, Rousseau goes on to compose the Ninth Walk as proof of his love for children. Because it is associated with a specific memory, that difficult theme can become the subject of a reverie. In this case, the memory has the advantage of demonstrating that, for him, the most exquisite happiness came only when it was shared with those around him.

Four or five years earlier, during a Sunday visit to the Bois de Boulogne, he and Thérèse were relaxing in the shade after lunch when a group of twenty young girls, perhaps orphans, supervised by a nun, arrived. As Rousseau watched their rambunctious play, they were joined by an *oublieur*. Probably an apprentice baker, the street vendor offered for sale the combined pleasures of a tasty cookie and a low-stakes lottery. Rather than sell these thin, cone-shaped cookies, the *oublieur* sold a chance to win one or many sweets. In addition to the basket of *oublies*, he carried a wooden box with a metal needle that could be spun over the surface of a dial divided into numbered sections. Where the needle came to rest indicated whether the prize was a single cookie, many cookies, or no cookie at all. As the vendor approached, the young girls crowded around him, as anxious to risk their few pennies as the nun was to put a stop to their foolishness. At this point Rousseau stepped forward and announced that he would pay for one spin by each of the girls: "Ce mot répandit dans toute la troupe une joye qui seule eut plus que payé ma bourse quand je l'aurois toute employée à cela" ("This word spread a joy through the whole group which alone would have more than reimbursed me, had I used up all my money"). Rousseau's role in this scene of joyful anticipation, however, doesn't stop there. To be sure that the children are not disappointed, Rousseau whispers to the vendor that he should "user de son adresse ordinaire en sens contraire" ("use his ordinary skill in an opposite sense"), so that each spin of the needle produces a winner. After all have had their turn, the twenty girls end up with almost a hundred cookies. Rousseau and Thérèse do what they can to encourage the luckier players to share their winnings with the less fortunate, but quarrels break out. Now Rousseau assumes the position of an authority ensuring that the common good is equally shared: "Pendant toute cette operation, il y eut des disputes qu'on porta devant mon tribunal . . . ces petites filles venant plaider tour à tour leur cause" ("During this whole operation, disputes arose which were brought before my tribunal . . . these little girls coming one after the other to plead their case"). Finally, this scene of joyous children, presided over by a scrupulous judge, produces for Rousseau the stuff of his most consoling reveries: "cette après midi fut une de celles de ma vie dont je me rapelle le souvenir avec le plus de satisfaction" (1091) ("that afternoon was one of those of my life which I remember with the greatest satisfaction" [82–83]).

The word *oublie* comes from the medieval Latin *oblata*, the past participle of the verb "to offer." In the eighteenth century, the word designated not only a type of cookie but an unconsecrated host, the wafer of unleavened bread that, in the Mass, would become for the faithful the body of Christ. The Mass, of course, is a transitive ritual, the commemoration of a redemption extending its salutary effect to all who participate in it. Rousseau, as he describes his Sunday in the Bois de Boulogne, becomes not only a version of the Lawgiver described in the *Contrat social* but also the guarantor of a gift that lifts him out of his self-enclosed solipsism. Like a secular Christ, he becomes the central figure in a ceremony that extends its happiness to the society of children around him: "Quand j'ai bien réflechi sur l'espéce de volupté que je goutois dans ces sortes d'occasions j'ai trouvé qu'elle consistoit moins dans un sentiment de bienfaisance que dans le plaisir de voir des visages contens" (1093) ("When I have carefully thought about the kind of sensual pleasure I savored on these occasions, I have found that it consisted less in a feeling of beneficence than in the pleasure of seeing contented faces" [84]).

On the first of the playing cards preserved in the Bibliothèque de Neuchâtel, Rousseau makes a surprising claim. Surveying his past life, he suddenly sees the real shape of his previous works: "Pour bien remplir le titre de ce recueil je l'aurois du commencer il y a soixante ans: car ma vie entiére n'a guére été qu'une longue réverie divisée en chapitres par mes promenades de chaque jour" (1165) ("To really live up to the title of this collection, I should have begun it sixty years ago: for my entire life has hardly been more than a long reverie divided into chapters by my daily walks" (my trans.). No longer the lone voice revealing to humankind a truth it will not recognize, Rousseau sees the sense of his life as a struggle to preserve those privileged and purifying moments that occurred only by chance in the lottery of life. Realizing this, he will write not as the narrator of synoptic histories but as the poet of an enchanted consciousness. Turning away from the degradations of life in society, the sentient individual, directly in contact with nature and innocence, discovers an ecstasy limited to the chance epiphanies of the instant.

Rousseau's lottery in the Bois de Boulogne reveals the tension that lies at the core of the *Rêveries*. Attempting to preserve in writing a happiness kept safe from the hostility of others, Rousseau must still find some way of reaching out to those around him. Now, rather than as the narrator of a hidden history, he will achieve such contact with others only in chance encounters like the one that allowed him to share the giddy joy of innocent children showered with cookies in his staged lottery. The *Rêveries* presents, in ten unintegrated walks, the final reflections of a consciousness grappling with the contradictions of a goodness it sees as innate, a responsibility to truth it sees as unswerving, and a persecution it sees as implacable. Having failed at sharing the truth of his narratives, he is left to find happiness only in the rare ecstasy of the moment's chance.

Genre and Feminine Duplicity in the *Confessions*

Sarah Herbold

What makes the *Confessions* a "monument" of modern literature, as Rousseau himself calls it on the first page? Having begun in a grandiose style, Rousseau soon descends into the most minute—even "low"—details of everyday life. This alternation between "high" and "low" subjects and styles corresponds to a dichotomy of genre and gender that is central to the project of the *Confessions*. In the opening paragraphs, Rousseau defines his autobiography as an "enterprise without example" because, to an unprecedented degree, he will bring together his public and private selves and show the continuity between them. This moral and psychological undertaking has a literary corollary: Rousseau is trying to combine a canonical public genre, the memoir, with less traditional private forms such as diaries, letters, and novels. The memoir was typically written by a well-known statesman and assumed a male audience; it described historical deeds and, as an exemplary text, appealed to the reader's intellect and moral judgment. In contrast, diaries, letters, and especially novels (many of them epistolary), which were sometimes written by women and typically seemed to address a female readership, appealed to the sensibilities. These works described singular and ordinary events that transpired out of public view, and they toyed with the boundary between the real and the fictive. The title *Confessions* (rather than *Mon Portrait* or *Mémoires*, which Rousseau also considered) seems to designate a new combination: public, "masculine" genres and aspects of the self fused with private, "feminine" ones.

Scholars often describe the synthesis of the public and the private as one of Rousseau's major achievements. Jean Marie Goulemot, for example, writes that in the *Confessions* "the barrier between public and private has ceased to exist, as the private is exhibited in public." In consequence, a new kind of "bond is established between writer and reader. . . . The result is a pale but nonetheless real reflection of that transparency of hearts which is for Rousseau the distinguishing characteristic of primitive and not-yet-corrupted societies" (392). A faithful reading of the *Confessions* would thus reproduce something like Rousseau's ideal state of nature, in which private interest does not exist because what each individual knows, believes, desires, and does is acknowledged and shared by everyone. But I would suggest that Rousseau failed to make the public and the private faces of his autobiography coincide and, moreover, that this failure is what makes the *Confessions* a "monument" of modern literature. On the one hand, the gap between memoir and confessional novel vitiates Rousseau's self-representation and divides readers internally as well as from Rousseau, and from "society" (however imagined), even as it unites these participants in the textual world. On the other hand, the gap between memoir and novel is also responsible for the *Confessions*' singular psychological and literary innovations, for it forces—and allows—the reader to experience tensions between conflicting versions of truth and reality that characterize modern literature.

Rousseau sometimes acknowledges the gap between memoir and confessional novel, but he typically disowns it and projects it onto female sexuality. This maneuver is especially apparent in the account of his relation with "Maman" (in English, "Mamma"). The story of Maman is central to the *Confessions*, for Rousseau divides not only his life but also his text into two halves based on the date of his separation from her. Maman is partly mythical: always associated with the beauty and innocence of nature, she constitutes an Edenic world without limits, conflict, or boundaries. Within her confines, Rousseau says, he always felt at one with her, himself, and his surroundings (e.g., 52 [43–44]). Even the sexual relationship the two shared is integral to this innocent transparence; in proposing to make their relationship a sexual one, Rousseau says, Maman was motivated solely by a desire to protect her young charge from the snares of other women. She herself lacked sexual passion and was totally unselfish (196–97 [164–65]). Similarly, Rousseau claims that he failed to experience real sexual pleasure with Maman (253–54 [212]).

In accordance with this myth, Rousseau describes Maman's "betrayal" in book 6 as unprecedented and inexplicable. It not only expels him from a paradise of innocence into a fallen world but also creates the very breach between the ideal and the actual that Rousseau spent the rest of his life trying to unwrite. The sign of Maman's fallen nature is sexuality itself—which Rousseau now attributes to her but not to himself. No longer an integral part of the mythical sublime union, Maman's sexuality is her original sin, as it were. Rousseau implies that Maman's decision to sleep with another man was the inevitable consequence of her earlier decision to make her relationship with Rousseau a sexual one (264 [221]). Sexuality, which is specifically feminine, inherently constitutes the fall from idyll (books 1–6) into history (books 7–12).

But this myth of woman as the fall does not accord very well with other narrative details. Most obvious are some all-too-human flaws that were always present in Maman. Periodically, Rousseau figuratively pulls aside the scarf that barely covered Maman's ample bosom (107 [89]) and lets the reader see that, all along, the real Maman was promiscuous, extravagant, greedy, manipulative, and deceptive. But Rousseau also sometimes reveals his own ambivalence and ulterior motives. For example, he acknowledges that even during the supposedly happy years he spent with Maman, he often preferred dreaming about her to being with her (181 [152]). He also admits that after meeting her, he retained "une humeur un peu volage, un desir d'aller et venir qui s'étoit plustot borné qu'éteint" (214) ("a slightly fickle mood, a desire to come and go that had been constrained rather than extinguished" [180]).

In fact, although the intimacy between Rousseau and Maman dominates the first half of the autobiography thematically, Rousseau devotes far more space to recounting the various ways in which that intimacy was interrupted.

The cataclysm at the end of book 6, for example, is preceded by a long story of a six-week affair Rousseau himself had with a married mother of ten children who was twenty years older than he. This affair occurred during one of Rousseau's many lengthy trips away from Maman, this one to Montpellier, where he was supposed to be seeking a cure for his mysterious illnesses. Regarding these trips, Rousseau declares, "Les pretextes ne me manquoient pas pour tous ces voyages" (215) ("I did not lack pretexts for all these trips" [180]). The word "pretextes," of course, signals that in hindsight—and perhaps also at the time—Rousseau recognizes that while Maman may have managed her relation with Petit ("Little One," as she called Rousseau) to suit her own complex needs, Petit did the same with her.

We can see how integral "feminine" duplicity is to the writing of the *Confessions*, as well as to the content of the work, in scenes such as the one in which Rousseau recounts his return from Montpellier. In book 6, Rousseau relates how, as he left Montpellier, he was not sure whether he wanted to go to Bourg-Saint-Andéol and continue his affair with Mme de Larnage or return to Maman at Chambéry. Representing himself as a kind of Augustinian prodigal son, he claims that he experienced a moral crisis that made him resolve to return to Maman. Ironically, a fatal "chain of misfortunes" had already been set in motion:

> Helas! la sincérité de mon retour au bien sembloit me promettre une autre destinée; mais la mienne étoit ecrite et déja commencée, et quand mon cœur plein d'amour pour les choses bonnes et honnêtes ne voyoit plus qu'innocence et bonheur dans la vie, je touchois au moment funeste qui devoit trainer à sa suite la longue chaine de mes malheurs.   (260)

> Alas! the sincerity of my return to good seemed to promise me a different destiny; but mine was written and already begun, and if my heart—full of love for good and decent things—no longer saw anything but innocence and happiness in life, I was touching the fatal moment that must drag the long chain of my misfortunes after it.   (218)

This expostulation is in the high style of Racinian tragedy: a flawed but repentant hero is about to be cruelly struck down by fate. In the next paragraph, however, Rousseau relates that on this occasion, as he had often done before, he strategically delayed his return so as to arrive at the exact hour when he had written to Maman to expect him. He did this, he reveals, because Maman always arranged a "petite fête" ("little holiday") to celebrate his return. He confides, "ces empressemens qui m'étoient si sensibles valoient bien la peine d'être menagés" (261) ("these attentions, which were so gratifying to me, were well worth the trouble of arranging" [218]). Rousseau thus reveals that he sought to maximize both his protection within Maman's confines and his freedom from her by aggravating the tension between them. Here we are in the world of the novel, in which hidden motivations and seemingly banal details fascinate the reader.

Rousseau manages his narrative in the same way that he managed his return from Montpellier. He creates novelistic suspense as he describes what happened when he reached Maman's house:

> J'arrivai donc exactement à l'heure. De tout loin je regardois si je ne la verrois point sur le chemin; le cœur me battoit de plus en plus à mesure que j'approchois. J'arrive [Rousseau switches to the present tense] essoufflé, car j'avois quitté ma voiture en ville : je ne vois personne dans la cour, sur la porte, à la fenêtre; je commence à me troubler; je redoute quelque accident. J'entre; tout est tranquille; des ouvriers goutoient [tense change] dans la cuisine; du reste aucun apprêt. La servante parut surprise de me voir, elle ignoroit que je dusse arriver. Je monte [tense change], je la vois enfin, cette chere Maman si tendrement, si vivement, si purement aimée; j'accours je m'élance à ses pieds. Ah! te voila, petit! me dit-elle en m'embrassant : as-tu fait bon voyage? comment te portes-tu? Cet accueil m'interdit [tense change] un peu. Je lui demandai si elle n'avoit pas receu ma lettre? Elle me dit qu'oui. J'aurois cru que non, lui dis-je; et l'éclaircissement finit-là. Un jeune homme étoit avec elle. Je le connoissois pour l'avoir vu déja dans la maison avant mon départ : mais cette fois il y paroissoit établi, il l'étoit. Bref je trouvai ma place prise.   (261)

Thus I arrived exactly on time. From far away I looked to see if I might not see her on the road; my heart beat more and more as I drew near. I arrive [Rousseau switches to the present tense] out of breath, for I had left my carriage in the city: I see no one in the courtyard, at the door, at the window; I begin to get flustered; I dread some accident. I enter; everything is calm; some workers were snacking [tense change] in the kitchen; otherwise no preparations. The maid appeared surprised to see me, she did not know that I was supposed to arrive. I go [tense change] upstairs, at last I see her, that dear Mamma so tenderly, so keenly, so purely loved; I run up I throw myself at her feet. "Ah! here you are little one!" she says to me while embracing me. "Have you had a good trip? How are you?" This welcome bewildered [tense change] me a little. I asked her if she had not received my letter. She told me yes. "I would have thought not," I said to her; and explanations ended there. A young man was with her. I knew him because I had already seen him in the house before my departure: but this time he appeared established there, indeed he was. In short I found my place taken.

(218–19)

Two versions of this incident clash before the reader's eyes: one in which Rousseau is the innocent victim of Maman's betrayal and of fate, and another in which a complicated dynamic of collaboration and antagonism between two equally skillful and ambivalent parties has finally reached a crisis. A striking contrast is also evident between the detailed narrative describing this scene of arrival and the tragic rhetoric that immediately precedes it. The reader can't be sure whether the narrative detail is meant to make the preceding bombast seem like self-parody—rather, Rousseau seems to be suggesting that his discovery of Maman's "infidelity" really was an unforeseen disaster. Nonetheless, the contrast between the two styles (and the two views of the world they represent) tarnishes his earlier portrait of himself as the victim of fate and makes it almost comic. As narrator, that is, Rousseau is in the same precarious position he was in as lover: he is at once in control of a duplicitous situation and powerless over it. He invites his audience to read suspiciously but also forbids them to do so.

This narrative double-b(l)ind is as deliberately inadvertent as Rousseau's predicament in Maman's house. The writer's correspondence reveals that he knew, before he left for Montpellier, that Wintzenried had taken his place and that Rousseau had probably left Chambéry in order to forestall just such a crisis as the one he describes here (*OC* 1: 1361n1). Indeed, even in the quotation cited here, Rousseau mentions that he had seen Wintzenried at Maman's before he went to Montpellier. Thus, although he has chosen to dramatize the incident in such a way as to lend credence to the myth of the fall, the conflicts in his account produce something much more "interesting" (in the sense of investing the text with a "private interest"). In alternating passages, the reader switches back and forth from experiencing the event as Rousseau himself supposedly did on that morning to viewing it with the detachment of Rousseau the narrator, reflecting on an incident long past. Such complex—and conflicting—representations of time, intention, knowledge, and point of view are characteristic of the modern novel.

The sense of external loss is also compensated by an internal gain, which is both existential and literary. Existentially, it was precisely this separation from Maman that made Rousseau an enterprising individual. He was forced to go to Paris to seek his fortune—which he would do in terms of textual rather than monetary capital and which he had long been contemplating. Literarily, Rousseau's sense that he has been irretrievably cut off from the metaphysical unity whose illusion, at least, had sustained him during his years with Maman puts him (and the reader) in the center of a new, novelistic world. He arrives at "exactly the right moment" ("exactement à l'heure"), only to find that the climax is a (climactic) anticlimax. There is neither tragedy nor comedy; rather, time is an indifferent continuum, and the moment has meaning only in wholly individual terms. But the absence of dramatic structure makes possible a Flaubertian foregrounding of immediate sensory experience that is a hallmark of the modern novel.

It is no coincidence that the scene of Rousseau's discovery that he has been suddenly ousted from the atemporal and preindividuated realm of myth (and memoir) into the time-bound and solipsistic world of fiction is one of the most strikingly novelistic passages in the *Confessions*. For the intersection of life and work and of personal and historical transformation that generally characterizes Rousseau's writings is nowhere more evident than in this scene, in which Rousseau as autobiographer manipulates the formal and thematic oppositions that structured his experience—and that of his era—as he describes how he manipulated similar oppositions in his life. Rousseau shows how, through his interactions with Maman, he plays with temporal, spatial, and psychological divisions between differing versions of himself in a way that belies his pretensions to simplicity. At key moments, the myth of the fall from unity into division, and of Maman as the cause of that fall, is exposed as precisely that: a myth. Instead, Maman appears as a kind of permeable medium, or hymen, through which Rousseau "managed" the movement between private and public selves, worlds, and genres that makes the *Confessions* a "monument" of duplicity.

All these forms of "management" had the same goal: Rousseau sought to generate himself as the originator of a literary form. The scene of what Rousseau describes as a catastrophic discovery can be juxtaposed with a fragment Rousseau had composed many years before he began to write his autobiography. In "Sur les evénements dont les femmes ont été la cause secrette" (*OC* 2: 1257–59), he envisions the creation of a genre he calls *histoire*. The fragment's thesis is that history as ordinarily defined—namely, the record of the deeds of famous men—is nothing more than a pack of impressive lies. It is women, he declares, not men, who are the real makers of history. From behind the scenes, women skillfully manage the private passions and intrigues that motivate men to alter the course of events. A real *histoire* could be written only by someone who could connect these "low," hidden details with the lofty public events that were determined by them. Such a historian would mediate not only between private and public life but also between the secret world of women and the self-trumpeting world of men. By necessity, this writer would be androgynous and equivocal, and the narrative would be formally unstable.

In "Sur les evénements," Rousseau declares that he lacks the talent to write this kind of feminine *histoire*. But in the *Confessions*, he chronicles his self-parturition as the originator of a narrative of "feminine" duplicity.

The Mechanics of Language:
Personification in the *Rêveries*

Virginia E. Swain

The *Rêveries* has been called the "autobiography of philosophy," an account of Rousseau's unique life, written not for itself but as the basis for "reflecting on life as a whole" (Davis 6). I do not mean to quarrel with the argument that the *Rêveries* is a philosophical work that encourages us to extrapolate from Rousseau's example to larger issues affecting us all. But I do take exception to the underlying premise that Rousseau's life is a given. That life is created on the page, in the writing of the *Rêveries* and Rousseau's other autobiographies, and we miss a crucial step when we overlook the laws of language that make this creation possible. Writing (or, more basically, language) is an integral part of autobio-*graphy* (from *graphein*, "to write") and one of the conditions enabling the creation of any life story.

This essay examines some philosophical implications of the role of language in the creation of Rousseau's life. In particular, I look at the rhetorical figure of personification, which attributes personal characteristics to inanimate objects or abstract notions. Personification is the means by which philosophical ideas are represented in the form of human beings. If we want to understand the philosophical ramifications of Rousseau's life, we must take into account this crucial link. Furthermore, as we learn to be attentive to words and rhetoric in individual texts, we become more astute readers, not just of Rousseau but of our (written and spoken) world.

Rousseau takes up the subject of personification in a curious paragraph (par. 13) in the Eighth Walk, where he declares its use unwise. People who personify the cause of their misfortunes, he says, deepen their misery. Because personal insult is much more damaging than physical harm, the best way to remain sanguine about misfortune is not to blame others. Rather than attribute the unhappy events in life to others' malevolent intentions, individuals should consider their troubles to be the effects of chance.

Rousseau gives two illustrations. A gambler, devastated by his losses and with no one to blame, imagines that fate has her "eyes" on him and intends to torment him; but this idea distresses him even more. A wise man, in contrast, is not upset by misfortune; he accepts "les coups de l'aveugle nécessité" (1078) ("the blows of blind necessity" [72]) and its role in his life.

Rousseau has apparently applied this lesson to his own situation. Instead of struggling to understand the inscrutable behavior of his persecutors, he has decided to view them as purely mechanical bodies, propelled by the laws of motion and devoid of any intent to do him harm (par. 12). Reduced to "machines," his enemies may strike him, but as accidents caused by moving bodies, these random events have little lasting effect on his emotions.

This passage on personification is quirky and dense. In the example of the gambler, Rousseau explicitly names chance (and loss) as the impetus behind personification, while personification works to oppose chance by attributing deliberate intent to others. Chance is the irrational problem that personification is called on to overcome. But in the example of the wise man and in Rousseau's own case, chance is the remedy for the irrational behavior that personification promotes. Chance is alternately a problem and a cure—and so is personification.

This short passage raises many questions about the value, effects, and function of personification, especially in a work that makes such frequent use of it. Rousseau presents personification as a deliberate choice. He claims that a wise man can remain calm in the face of adversity by deciding not to personify his fate. But in the examples that illustrate the wisdom of rejecting personification, personification persists, not only in the persons of the gambler and the wise man but also in the figures of "(sighted) fate" and "blind necessity." Personification comes back by chance, it seems, just when Rousseau expresses the intention to eliminate it. Does Rousseau completely control this device, or does personification impose itself in a random or "mechanical" way?

The possibility that persons are created as a necessary and unwilled effect of language would have far-reaching consequences for the usual reading of the *Rêveries* as the rendering of true-life events.

Personification is bound up, in the Eighth Walk, with the problem of causality. Rousseau postulates and examines, in turn, two possible causes of the misfortunes that have beset him, attributing them either to persons acting deliberately or to mechanical laws acting as random forces in his life. In other words, he alternately personifies or mechanizes fate, and he tries to be clear about the difference between the two.

Rousseau's primary focus is on understanding what prompts people to behave as they do. However, he quickly abandons his attempt to explain his enemies' attitudes and actions; he concludes that their judgments are not based on rational principles but on passions and the prejudices that follow from them. Their actions may be willed, but their will is not informed by any logic; they are caught up in "le plus inique et absurde système qu'un esprit infernal put inventer" ("the most iniquitous and absurd system an infernal mind could invent"). In essence, whatever their will or intent, their behavior is ultimately "l'effet du hazard" (1077) ("the effect of chance" [72, 71]).

The absence of any connection between principled thought and people's actions drives Rousseau to depersonify his fate. Instead of scrutinizing his enemies' hearts and minds, he looks to physics for an explanation of their behavior. If people engage in actions that are not grounded in the laws of logic or morality, then they must be acting on impulse; so, in an amusing twist, Rousseau imputes their actions to the laws of motion. He decides to view people as nothing more than bodies or masses, devoid of any knowable innerness and subject only to the laws uncovered by Newton: "Je ne vis plus en eux que des masses différemment mues, depourvues à mon égard de toute moralité" (1078) ("I no longer saw in them anything but randomly [differently] moved masses, destitute of all morality with respect to me" [72]).

If personification implies innerness, logic, and meaning, senseless events cannot be personified; they must be merely mechanical. By means of this shift, Rousseau transforms what he sees as the arbitrary, impulsive behavior of his enemies into a physical law. Put another way, he converts random acts into a kind of necessity and, in so doing, brings them back within the reach of understanding. "Impulsion" ("impulse") is no longer an unforseeable psychological phenomenon, but a property of bodies in motion: "je compris que mes contemporains n'étoient par rapport à moi que des êtres méchaniques qui n'agissoient que par impulsion et dont je ne pouvois calculer l'action que par les loix du mouvement" (1078) ("I understood that in relation to me my contemporaries were nothing more than automatons who acted only on impulse and whose action I could calculate only from the laws of motion" [72]).

However, the problem of causality is not completely solved for Rousseau, who wishes to harden himself against the machinations of his enemies by finding some necessity in their behavior. For inert bodies may be set into motion by very different forces (impersonal and personal), as Rousseau recognizes when he speaks of "des masses différemment mues." Winds may wrest a slate tile from a roof and propel it to the ground, but the same tile may also be hurled by an individual intent on doing harm: "Une tuile qui *tombe d'un toit* peut nous blesser davantage mais ne nous navre pas tant qu'une pierre *lancée à dessein* par une main malveillante" (1078; emphasis added) ("A shingle *falling off a roof* can injure us more, but does not grieve us as much as a stone *thrown on purpose* by a malevolent hand" [72]). Despite his efforts to ascribe causality to mechanics alone, Rousseau has trouble removing persons from his explanations.

Rousseau wants to convert a series of inexplicable events into a necessary fact of life, by both playing on and attempting to erase the double meaning of "impulsion." But language has its own laws and is not so easily controlled. Rousseau may deliberately stress the idea that "impulse" is a purely physical phenomenon that can be predicted, but the notion that "impulse" is an unpredictable human urge persists despite his efforts. The difference between "impulse" as physical law and "impulse" as random psychological event makes all the difference to Rousseau, since it guarantees his own indifference to events; yet he is unable to keep the two apart. Simultaneously designating two very different types of phenomena, the word "impulse" has an uncontrollable tendency toward personification.

In fact, personification is not a technique systematically chosen or willed by the author; it is part of language's incontrovertible "mechanics." The referential shift from one idea of "impulse" to another is not subject to individual control. Necessary and unavoidable, personification can be set in motion by an "impulse" of language, acting without a cause. The example of the gambler personifying fate highlights this fact. The personification of chance imputes inscrutable and arbitrary intentions to a human figure and thus carries forward the theme of the impulsivity of human subjects; but it also suggests the controlling role of fate (or necessity) in personification itself. As Donald Davie remarks:

> "[P]ersonification," far from being a device that we may or may not avail ourselves of as we please, implies one rather alarming image of what sort of world it is that we live in. Either that world is by and large "up to us"; or else it is not. And personification implies that it is not.
>
> (103)

Rousseau is unable to hold apart personification and mechanics; he cannot keep one "impulse" from contaminating the other. However, this inescapable law of language, which poses a problem in the first part of the Walk, becomes a remedy in the Walk's last pages, where the mechanics of personification ultimately benefit the autobiographical hero.

In the last paragraphs of the Eighth Walk, the physical laws to which Rousseau imputed others' random acts reappear in a new, very personal context as the logical and necessary support for Rousseau's own behavior. The general outlines of his argument are already familiar from the example of "impulsion." Rousseau is an impulsive man, it seems, but this is the necessary consequence of his constitution, over which he has no control. His anger and indignation are the inevitable result of outside stimuli impacting on his exquisite senses, which in turn affect his passions. By connecting the laws of motion to his own physiology, Rousseau gives his body a new dimension. It has sensation and innerness, which the other bodies—considered as pure mass—lacked.

When an outside force strikes Rousseau's body, it sets his sensate and passionate being into motion. If Rousseau's eyes flash or his limbs tremble, it is beyond his control: "cela tient au seul physique" ("that is all purely physical"). Reason and will can neither cause nor govern these "mouvemens involontaires" (1083) ("involuntary motions" [76]). Rousseau's passions are the necessary and uncontrollable effect of the impact of an external stimulus on his senses. But this reaction also has an end:

> Tout vient également d'un tempérament versatile qu'un vent impetueux agite mais qui rentre dans le calme à l'instant que le vent ne souffle plus. C'est mon naturel ardent qui m'agite, c'est mon naturel indolent qui m'appaise. Je cede à toutes les impulsions présentes, tout choc me donne un mouvement vif et court, sitot qu'il n'y a plus de choc le mouvement cesse, rien de communiqué ne peut se prolonger en moi.   (1084)

Everything comes from a changeable temperament which is irritated by an impetuous wind, but becomes calm again the instant the wind stops blowing. My ardent natural temperament irritates me; my indolent natural temperament pacifies me. I yield to all present impulses; every conflict sets off an intense and short motion in me. As soon as the conflict subsides, the motion ceases.

(76–77; first sentence of trans. modified)

Like any mass, which moves only when a dynamic force is applied to it and returns to a state of rest when it is no longer impelled, Rousseau's body (considered in regard to his senses and his passions) is alternately active and agitated or slow-moving and lazy. His state of being depends on the presence or absence of an outside motor force.

Because of his particular constitution, the only way to gain control is to give up the attempt at control. Here again reason and will have no part; there is no countervailing personal, moral force that can stand against natural law. The initial "explosion" simply runs its course until the body, no longer impelled to act, naturally comes to rest. In that moment, Rousseau claims, he becomes his true and "constant" self: "au prémier instant de relache je redeviens ce que la nature a voulu, c'est là . . . mon état le plus constant et celui par lequel . . . je goute un bonheur pour lequel je me sens constitué" (1084) ("But in the first instant of respite, I again become what nature wanted . . . this is my most constant condition and the one through which . . . I savor a happiness for which I feel myself constituted" [77]).

Outside forces eventually cease, and Rousseau then finds himself—at rest, unmoved by the impulses of other men, indifferent. Rousseau's excitable and impulsive side may be problematic, in that it allows others to control him, but it is also the necessary means by which motion carries him to a "constant" state. Motion makes possible Rousseau's natural, effortless passage from misery to the calm enjoyment of life (1076 [71]). Thanks to the laws of motion, he arrives at the state of equilibrium described early in the Walk (1077 [71]). In sum, the mechanical explanation results in the delineation of a man confident in his self-understanding and in his nature: "rend[u] à moi-même"(1084) ("come back to myself" [77]), "ce que la nature a voulu" ("what nature wanted"). Arriving at stasis in the world of motion is the equivalent of attributing stable properties, or a proper self, to Rousseau, the hero of this narrative.

But this is not first and foremost a personal tale. The human story elaborated in the Eighth Walk is instead an effect of the very rhetorical shift within language that we earlier described. Motion is communicated in this Walk not only by the theme of physical laws but through the active laws of language. The entire Eighth Walk is predicated on the double referentiality of its key words—*mouvement, impétueux, choc*, and *impulsion*—which designate the physical phenomena characteristic of the external world of objects as well as the inner psychological workings of human beings. The simultaneous reference to these diverse fields of action creates the necessary condition for establishing an analogy between them, an analogy that therefore seems perfectly natural. The chance collision of the divergent senses of these words sets into motion the transfer of meaning from one register to another, which in turn allows the narrative of Rousseau's about-face to unfold. Put another way, the laws of motion that account for the revolution in Rousseau's situation find an equivalent in language's own tropes (from the Greek *tropos*, "turn"). His own "tempérament versatile" ("changeable temperament") embodies—in the agitation of his senses and their subsequent repose—the "versatility" of language. Rousseau, the hero of these pages, personifies (the mechanics of) personification.

The Perceptual Metamorphosis
of the Solitary Walker

John C. O'Neal

In early 1776, after some twelve years of cultivating the art of botanizing, Jean-Jacques Rousseau suddenly drops this pastime. He no longer feels that it is useful (*Rêv.* 1060 [57]). His withdrawal from botanizing seems final. Despite his protestations to the contrary in his *Lettres sur la botanique* (1771–73), Rousseau now believes that this hobby demands a strong memory, which he no longer has. Nevertheless, in 1777, more than a year later, he returns to it with renewed vigor (1061 [57]).

Two Walks in Rousseau's *Rêveries*, namely the Fifth and the Seventh, deal extensively with his botanizing and, when compared, reveal the causes underlying his change in attitude. In establishing certain modes of perception as significant aspects of his hobby, each Walk has a distinct emphasis. The Fifth Walk stresses a rational kind of observation, whereas the Seventh Walk gives vent to what one might call sensual observation, in which the beholder is concerned primarily with external form and sensations. In the earlier Walk, Rousseau seeks in nature the same order and harmony he wishes to find in himself. Not until the later Walk, however, does he discover, and indeed delight in, a certain relation to nature that leads him to a new awareness of his consciousness—which, like the one we have come to accept as our own in modern times, is based not on unity and sameness but on multiplicity and difference.

In the Fifth Walk, Rousseau describes, in a celebrated passage, the ideal state of consciousness he would like to attain permanently:

> un état où l'ame trouve une assiete assez solide pour s'y reposer tout entiére et rassembler là tout son être, sans avoir besoin de rappeller le passé ni d'enjamber sur l'avenir; où le tems ne soit rien pour elle, où le présent dure toujours sans neanmoins marquer sa durée et sans aucune trace de succession, sans aucun autre sentiment de privation ni de jouissance, de plaisir ni de peine, de desir ni de crainte que celui seul de notre existence. . . . (1046)

> a state in which the soul finds a solid enough base to rest itself on entirely and to gather its whole being into, without needing to recall the past or encroach upon the future; in which time is nothing for it; in which the present lasts forever without, however, making its duration noticed and without any trace of time's passage; without any other sentiment of deprivation or of enjoyment, pleasure or pain, desire or fear, except that alone of our existence. . . . (46)

It is from this so-called sentiment of existence that Rousseau derived great happiness on the Island of Saint-Pierre. Marked as it is by a lack of succession and an absence of temporality, this fixed state appears to circumvent the anguish caused by the continual flux of things on earth.

Botany first attracts Rousseau because it necessitates a rational observation that can give a momentary sense of fixity to things and to the self. Its preoccupation with detail ultimately leads to a comprehensive idea of nature. From the study of an individual phenomenon, one can acquire a unified sense of nature, which for Rousseau would carry over into a unified sense of self. While on the Island of Saint-Pierre, he undertakes the exhaustive project of scrutinizing and describing every plant there. In the Fifth Walk he relates his plans for a *Flora petrinsularis*. He wants not only to describe plants in utmost detail but also to study their structure. In both cases, he engages in more than just observing in a sensual way. He must call upon reflection to help him make judgments about nature. In wishing to participate in the great order of nature, he chooses, in part, to observe it rationally, since mere sensations tend to remain separate unless unified by a deeper understanding. He must go beyond sensation and feeling to ideas. Rousseau himself is stupefied by his predilection for this activity, which seems to run counter to his normal penchant for attractions based more on feeling than on reason (1043 [43]).

Rational perception can yield a certain overview of nature's order and entices Rousseau into believing for a moment that he has at last found stability and happiness. He attempts to incorporate nature's unity into a project that he himself will produce—the herbarium (*herbier*). Theoretically, this book of dead leaves will link Rousseau to a solid force and give him, as author of the much smaller work, the claim to a certain unity, too. But ultimately the herbarium does not appeal to Rousseau by encouraging him to engage in further abstractions. To the contrary, Rousseau chooses in the herbarium a concrete form as a storehouse for his sensations in nature. As an object itself, it requires less mediation than would be necessitated by an operation that took place exclusively in his mind. He can refer to it at any time and recall whatever pleasant experience he had in observing the plants in the first place. It proves particularly useful once Rousseau leaves the countryside (1073 [67]). A small book suffices to give Rousseau a feeling for the entirety of nature.

It is noteworthy that the only endeavor Rousseau voluntarily cultivates in his old age is botanizing. Unlike reverie, this activity can actually be practiced. Since it can eventually yield the happiness he is seeking above all else, it constitutes for Rousseau one of the highest levels of wisdom. The wisdom about which Rousseau speaks in the Third Walk consists in learning how to implement in old age the lessons about happiness assimilated over a lifetime (1011 [17])

But in Rousseau's own late years, a basic change takes place. One mode of perception yields to another. Order, sameness, and stability give way to disorder, differences, and flux. Persuaded that happiness consists in "un état simple et permanent" (1046) ("a simple and permanent state" [45]), Rousseau had originally despaired of finding it: "Tout est dans un flux continuel sur la terre: rien n'y garde une forme constante et arrêtée, et nos affections qui s'attachent aux choses extérieures passent et changent necessairement comme elles. . . . il n'y a rien là de solide à quoi le cœur se puisse attacher" (1046) ("Everything is in continual flux on earth. Nothing on it retains a constant and static form, and our affections, which are attached to external things, necessarily pass away and change as they do. . . . There is nothing solid there to which the heart might attach itself" [46]). Approaching botany from a rational perspective can give at least a brief sense of stability to things and to the self. Eventually, however, this method of proceeding fails to procure for Rousseau the ultimate goal of personal happiness that depends much more on the feeling of his existence than on the knowledge of it. In his herbaria he may have faithfully gathered a large number of plants into a given pattern, but any mold crumbles before the organic whole of nature.

In the Seventh Walk, Rousseau modifies botanizing's rigid adherence to a single object, as presented in the Fifth Walk. The Seventh Walk dwells much less on the role of reason in the process of botanizing. Rousseau loses his desire for learning and instruction (1068 [64]). It is the flux of nature itself that concerns him here. His method consists in using his innate means for recognizing change—his sensations.

Rousseau's reappraisal of the sensations accounts, in large part, for the newness of his vision in the Seventh Walk and his different attitude toward botany: "un instinct qui m'est naturel . . . me fit pour la prémiére fois détailler le spectacle de la nature, que je n'avois guére contemplé jusqu'alors qu'en masse et dans son ensemble" (1062) ("An instinct which is natural to me . . . made me consider in detail for the first time the spectacle of nature which until then I had hardly contemplated except in a mass and in its wholeness" [59]). Whereas formerly he had bypassed the details of nature in his haste to derive a more comprehensive and rational idea of it, now he devotes his time specifically to the details. Although guided by a certain reasoning that differentiates between pleasure and pain, the senses are now given free rein to wander in nature. Indeed, by letting his senses go about from place to place, rather than keeping them fixed, Rousseau manages, finally, to come to grips with the problem posed by his desire for happiness in a permanent state. (Cf. Gusdorf 131–36, 433–39. The search for happiness parallels that for self-knowledge. The inwardness and the inaction of consciousness need a support in externalized experience.)

From a comparison between the Fifth and the Seventh Walks, we discover that Rousseau vacillates between two aspects of sensual observation. It can tend toward either a concentration or an atomization of attention. In the Fifth Walk, Rousseau concentrates on one sensory detail, the lapping of the water. Focusing his attention in this way allows him to go into a state of reverie, since it "captivates" his senses (1045 [45]). In this case, Rousseau valorizes concentration on one object. By its preoccupation with minutiae, botanizing separates sensations and facilitates such attention. And yet on other occasions, Rousseau's observations engage him in a cumulative process—for example, he attempts to approximate the diversity of nature in his small herbarium (1061 [58]). Whether his observing leads him to a concentration or an atomization of his gaze, it ultimately brings about a state of reverie. During his strolls through the fields, however, Rousseau gives less primacy, especially in the Seventh Walk, to the focusing of his senses on any one object than to the multiplicity of glances he casts about him. This perceptual approach to nature is facilitated by what may perhaps best be called itinerant botanizing: inaction yields to action.

For Rousseau, walking is of the utmost importance. That he calls the chapters in the *Rêveries* Walks and that he views himself as a walker (*promeneur*) are scarcely haphazard occurrences. What does remain unpredictable is Rousseau's behavior during these excursions, for he walks in no set pattern. Here Rousseau rejoins one of the key themes of his century—*le hasard*, or "random chance." Yet rather than consider chance an ordeal, he cleverly puts it to good use. So long as Rousseau stays alone in nature, it matters little what falls within his visual field. In fact, the greater the diversity and the disorder of the objects he sees, the greater the pleasure he derives. To feel nature's diversity, Rousseau himself must wander about, or, at least, his eyes must "walk around" a fertile terrain teeming with objects:

> J'errois nonchalemment dans les bois et dans les montagnes, n'osant penser de peur d'attiser mes douleurs. Mon imagination qui se refuse aux objets de peine laissoit mes sens se livrer aux impressions légéres mais douces des objets environnans. Mes yeux se promenoient sans cesse de l'un à l'autre, et il n'étoit pas possible que dans une varieté si grande il ne s'en trouvât qui les fixoient davantage et les arrêtoient plus long-tems. (1063)

> I would wander at random through the woods and mountains, not daring to think for fear of stirring up my sufferings. My imagination, which rejects sorrowful objects, let my senses give themselves up to the light but sweet impressions of surrounding objects. My eyes incessantly strayed from one object to another, and in such a great variety it was impossible not to find something which would captivate them more and hold them for a longer time. (59)

Although from these observations Rousseau does not glean an ideal immediate feeling, "cette recreation des yeux" (1063) ("this ocular recreation" [59]) allows him to stabilize his senses. Paradoxically, their greatest activity can also produce an immobilizing effect.

Notwithstanding the shortcomings of observing, Rousseau derives consolation from the plants themselves, the primary objects of botany. Although perhaps not immediately accessible to our souls, plants lie within our reach. They provide, he says, an open book whose existence seems to bespeak a providential hand (1069 [64]). The proximity of plants to humans facilitates an observation of them that leads to earthly happiness. All too often, human beings look to distant places, such as the stars, or seek in dark, hidden spots, such as jewel-producing mines, for their happiness. True pleasure, according to Rousseau, is much more easily attainable. We have only to look "sous nos pieds" (1069) ("under our feet" [64]).

Nature's diversity and Rousseau's sensationist tendency (see O'Neal, *Authority* 182–95) complement each other here. During the course of his walks, Rousseau comes to appreciate the immense variety in nature. He experiences this same effect whether he concentrates on a single atom of a plant, with the aid of his magnifying glass, or breaks up his gaze across a vast horizon of nature's creations. In the one case, the differences become all the more perceptible as the levels of magnification increase. In the other, he has only to walk through rural settings to savor their diversity. The scenes, however, must not be barren and must teem with pleasant objects (1062 [59]). In both cases, he is struck by the multiplicity and variety of nature, and his senses intensify his awareness of the abundance around him. The constitutive powers of the mind temporarily suspended, sensual observation replaces the perceptual investigations grounded in reason that Rousseau practiced earlier. Rather than strive to reorder and enclose the universe, however, sensual observation opens itself to nature's infinite possibilities. Rousseau never tires of exploring nature's three realms (plants, animals, and minerals). And yet the more he observes, the less he finds himself in nature. A curious metamorphosis occurs in him.

From the overwhelming sense of many outside him in nature, Rousseau feels oneness of self. In the *Rêveries*, Rousseau is less a natural man than a man in nature. There is a fundamental split between him and nature. The mythical identity between the two is gone but can be regained through reverie (1062–63 [59]). Rousseau's attitude toward nature undergoes a slight reorientation in the *Rêveries*. Instead of identifying with it at first, he posits his differences from it to such an extent that he becomes able to feel his self as *other* than nature.

Botanizing can create an experience similar to reverie. In fact, toward the end of the *Rêveries*, it has every indication of replacing it: "Le recueil de mes longs rêves est à peine commencé, et déja je sens qu'il touche à sa fin. Un autre amusement lui succede, m'absorbe, et m'ôte même le tems de rêver" (1060) ("The collection of my long dreams is scarcely begun, and I already feel it is near its end. Another pastime takes its place, absorbs me, and even deprives me of the time to dream" [57]). At this point, Rousseau finds the worth of sensual observation, a mode of perception that heretofore has received less than favorable acclaim because of its tendency to lead to self-absorption and vice. He champions it through the botanizing experience that emphasizes, above all else, movement. If Rousseau had lived longer, he would probably have dedicated himself to botany in its more mobile form. Reverie prompted from within would take second place to a botanizing that produces reverie from without, simply because the former runs the risk of inflaming his acute feelings of persecution, at the same time that his feelings of ecstasy are aroused. A good feeling can too easily give way to a haunting one (1062 [58–59]). Internalized reverie thus poses a danger that does not exist in itinerant botanizing. This latter activity, although superficially the opposite of reverie in that it keeps one firmly rooted in this world, actually produces similar results.

As reverie gives way to botanizing, a modification in the spatial and temporal schemes comes about. Reverie's eternal present finds its equivalent during Rousseau's botanizing expeditions. But the very idea of a lack of succession and temporality has changed. We no longer find the ideal of "a solid enough base" for the soul that Rousseau described in the Fifth Walk. The process of botanizing yields neither solid ground nor a lack of succession. With it, Rousseau depends on an infinite repetition of images. And as far as the eternal present is concerned, he must indulge in linking different moments in time. In going from one plant to the next, Rousseau gives himself a sense of nature's heterogeneity. By extension, he comes to a new awareness of his own sensations, which succeed each other in such rapid order that any view of the self as substantial or as the same at two distinct moments collapses.

The earlier movement from nature's minute detail to its totality reverses itself here. Rational perception reverts to the more sensual form, which allows Rousseau to go from a totality to nothing or, at most, to one small detail. The first step, however, requires an accumulation of sensations precipitated by unbridled observing of the sensual kind. It is precisely in that movement, which one scholar qualifies as "dangerous," that Rousseau must engage himself: "the experience of expansive fullness of the mind metamorphoses itself into its opposite, in an experience of dispersion in which the disappearing self tends to become absorbed and lost in the impalpable dust made up of the multitude of minute perceptible events" (Poulet 74). Rousseau's sense of the immensity of the universe derives precisely from the diversity of his sensations. He must lose himself in them (1062–63 [59]).

Each of his sensations in nature takes Rousseau away from the self. To arrive at degree zero of the self and a feeling for nature's vastness, he must infinitely increase his sensations (cf. Gouhier 104–07). Otherwise, he risks a reversion to the self (1084 [77]). His feeling of ecstasy—that is, those moments during which he stands the most *out* of this world—are those very moments during which he stands the most *in* this world. Rousseau must give himself over entirely to his sensations to effect his desired feelings. Although he may want one single uninterrupted moment of ecstasy, he can attain it only through many moments broken up by multiple gazes across nature's landscape.

What is crucial in this process is that Rousseau allows no space or time for the self. Only then does the self find a nothingness that is a cosmic fullness (Raymond, *La Quête de soi* 217). Nor does this event take place by a specifically directed negation of the self. It works indirectly—that is, by cause and effect, through, first and foremost, a heightening of the sensations during his botanizing and walks.

The Fifth Walk, in focusing on the means derived from within the self that allow for reverie, posits itself as an ideal. Rousseau refers to this reverie in a subsequent Walk, the Eighth, as a desired state. But the inner means of attaining it, touted in the Fifth Walk, can go bankrupt without warning. His faculties beginning to fail him, Rousseau cannot always depend on his memory to furnish images of previously experienced, fond reveries; hence the importance of the herbarium. His imagination no longer takes him as rapidly out of this world. Everything seems to indicate that the Fifth Walk may offer a glimpse of the desired solution, but it does not provide an everyday solution. As one writer notes, "it is a re-creation of the past rather than a concrete reality of the present" (Grimsley 296).

Nevertheless, the Seventh Walk more closely approximates the ideal, with its solution in the reality of nature. Rousseau takes up botanizing again, but with a different orientation this time. In conjunction with his strolls, botanizing will provide a fertile area for exploration. This moment comes after Rousseau has completed the *Lettres sur la botanique* and has sold his books, herbaria, and related paraphernalia. Rousseau may have a suspect tendency to claim many moments as unique, but in early summer 1777, he finds a newness in botanizing. The flux about which he complains in the Fifth Walk finds its antidote in change itself (cf. Starobinski, *Le Remède dans le mal*). Increasingly wary of his emotional feelings as a solid basis for the self, Rousseau, ironically, resorts to his sensations and their capacity to produce change. Few critics of Rousseau have seized on the central issue of sensation as lucidly as Basil Munteano: Rousseau, he says, abandons the dangerous vagaries of feeling in favor of physical sensibility and an attempted conquest of the inanimate universe. In the absolute solitude of sensation, Munteano believes, Rousseau finds his permanent self (72, 87). As in the unified image, or summary idea, he projects of himself in his previous autobiographical works, the Rousseau of the *Rêveries* generates unity of self through the multiplicity of his sensations across time. The state at which the solitary walker ultimately arrives, though perhaps not as solid and absolute as he had wished earlier, can make him sufficiently happy.

The Seventh Walk, inasmuch as it differs considerably from the Fifth, calls attention to the shift in emphasis from an inward orientation to an outward one. Rousseau, while appearing much less self-contained in the Seventh Walk, in fact needs nature and depends on it to provide him that feeling of nothingness whereby he attains the ultimate fullness of self. Dependent, he is also free, since he can "wander at random" in nature. Once again, we recognize a hallmark of Rousseau's: he juxtaposes moments, ideas, and states that appear, at first glance, utterly irreconcilable. And yet Rousseau embodies innumerable contradictions at the same time. In emptiness he finds fullness; in change, permanence. Observing, he can see once again in a way that he no longer thought possible.

NOTE

A version of this essay appeared in *L'Esprit Creatur* 24.2 (1984): 92–192. Used with permission.

The Public and the Self: Rousseau and Romanticism

Carl Fisher

The revolutionary undertones of the *Discours sur l'origine et les fondements de l'inégalité* and the *Contrat social*, in which Rousseau sees men in chains and argues that the *volonté générale* (general will) is part of the *ordre naturel* (natural order), clearly foreshadow radical Romantic thought. In this context the *Confessions* is more than a spiritual autobiography; it articulates the dissonance of the private individual's place in a dynamic public world. A modern reader will also recognize pivotal Romantic concerns: What is the relation of the self to society, and how should a writer define and represent the public?

The *Confessions* demonstrates the way concrete experience of injustice can produce revolutionary rhetoric. Rousseau propounds "l'enthousiasme de la vérité, de la liberté, de la vertu" (*OC* 1: 351) ("enthusiasm for truth, for freedom, for virtue" [*CW* 5: 295]) when he struggles with urban and social constraints; he sees only "oppression et misére dans notre ordre social" (416) ("oppression and misery in our social order" [349]) when he is alienated from the Republic of Letters. His mistreatment by the theater world leads to the *Discours sur l'inégalité*, Rousseau claims. In this work he reveals "les petits mensonges des hommes" (388) ("the petty falsehoods of men" [326]). Readers of Romantic texts should identify a forerunner of the social victim's heroic voice, especially in Rousseau's complaint that the world is deaf to his plaintive cry: "Insensés, qui vous plaignez sans cesse de la nature, aprenez que tous vos maux vous viennent de vous" (389) ("Madmen, who moan ceaselessly about nature, learn that all your ills come to you from yourselves" [326]). This passage, for example, mirrors the outrage of the creature in *Frankenstein* (1818), who is well aware of the injustice of cultural constructions yet remains marginalized and ostracized.

The *Confessions* also expresses Rousseau's frustration with draconian political power and artificial social hierarchy. He describes a reified world of privilege and closed social circles, with oblique origins, which characterized European society generally before the emergence in the later eighteenth century of what Jürgen Habermas has conceptualized as a public sphere typified by critical public debate. Rousseau attempts intellectually to sidestep social and political constraints by presenting idealized versions of the peasantry and of a countryside inhabited by "très bonnes gens" (146) ("very good people" [122]) who lack vanity and self-interest. The local folk impress Rousseau with their generous simplicity, and the difficulties of rural life spark his indignation. In book 4, after a day's outing, Rousseau enters a peasant's hut and at first receives poor fare but is treated to a veritable feast when the villager realizes that Rousseau is not an exciseman: "Ce fut là le germe de cette haine inextinguible qui se developpa depuis dans mon cœur contre les vexations qu'éprouve le malheureux peuple et contre ses oppresseurs" (164) ("That was the seed of that inextinguishable hatred that has developed in my heart since then against the vexations suffered by the unfortunate people and against its oppressors" [138]). Similarly, Goethe's *Sorrows of Young Werther* (1774) and Wordsworth and Coleridge in *Lyrical Ballads* (1798) idealize the peasantry and create narrative voices identified with the oppressed. Chateaubriand's *Atala* (1801) and Novalis's *Heinrich von Ofterdingen* (1802) likewise promote the countryside as a source of value. Rousseau's contention that many rural problems correlate directly to the preservation of aristocratic privilege (574 [481]) becomes a standard for later Romantics like Shelley and Heine.

Cosmopolitan life troubles Rousseau because cities are sites of corruption. In the *Confessions* he describes being initially drawn to urban spectacle but concludes that cities are dirty and dangerous places, as evident in his first impression of Paris:

> je ne vis que de petites rues sales et puantes, de vilaines maisons noires, l'air de la malpropreté, de la pauvreté, des mendians, des chartiers, des ravaudeuses, des crieuses de tisanne et de vieux chapeaux.   (159)

> I saw only filthy and stinking little streets, nasty-looking black houses, the air of dirtiness, poverty, beggars, carters, cobblers, vendors of rotgut and old hats.   (133)

Like most eighteenth-century thinkers, he recognizes urban settings and workplaces as a nexus of contention. He contrasts city dwellers with the rural folk and does not have the same sympathy for those who must make a living in confined and constrained circumstances. In general, Rousseau shows disdain for the conditions of working life—for example, when, as a young man, he is employed by the survey, he complains of the "plus maussade travail avec des gens encore plus maussades, enfermé dans un triste Bureau empuanti de l'haleine et de la sueur de tous ces manans, la pluspart fort mal peignés et fort malpropres" (188) ("gloomy work with still gloomier people, closed up in a sad Office stinking with the breath and sweat of all these boors, the majority extremely unkempt and extremely dirty" [158]). He despises the urban experience, as many Romantics will, critiquing everything from the pace of life to the lack of community. What distresses Rousseau in particular is the conflict between personal will and public activity that eventually characterizes the public sphere. He longs for the country, far from "l'urbaine cohuë" (374) ("the urban throng" [314]).

To Rousseau, daily urban life is vexatious; he presents extraordinary events as even more disturbing. On hearing "du trouble et de l'agitation qui régnoient dans Paris" ("about the trouble and agitation that reigned in Paris"), he says, "combien je remerciai le Ciel de m'avoir éloigné de ces spectacles d'horreurs et de crimes, qui n'eussent fait que nourrir, qu'aigrir l'humeur bilieuse que l'aspect des desordres publics m'avoit donnée" (437–38) ("how much did I thank Heaven for having kept me away from these spectacles of horrors and crimes which would have done nothing but nourish, but sharpen, the bilious mood which the sight of public disorders has given me" [368]). Always conscious of potential popular disorder, he mentions revolutionary activity in Turin (176 [148]), agitation in Rouen (538 [450]), and "le mécontentement général du peuple et de tous les ordres de l'Etat" (565) ("the general discontent of the people and of all the orders of the State" [473]) in 1761 in France. Civil war is a "spectacle affreux" ("horrible spectacle") in which brothers cut each other's throats; he vows "ne tremper jamais dans aucune guerre civile, et de ne soutenir jamais au dedans la liberté par les armes ni de ma personne ni de mon aveu" (216) ("never to be a party to any civil war, and never to uphold domestic freedom with arms, or my person, or my assent" [181]). Elsewhere Rousseau argues that the people have the right to rebel when mistreated, and many of his ideas inspire revolutionaries, but the *Confessions* shows that Rousseau does not have revolution at heart. The sense of outrage at the corruption and collusion of nobility and public officials that can lead to revolt—and thus to intolerable civil unrest—finds exemplary Romantic representation in Heinrich von Kleist's *Michael Kohlhaas* (1810), which dramatizes the critical drawbacks of popular disorder and concludes that public order supersedes individual rights.

Rousseau's ambivalence about the public suggests a correspondence between author, work, and audience that will be characteristic of the Romantic writer. Rousseau laments that he can control neither the way he is seen in the world nor the way in which his works will be interpreted. The phrase "yeux du public" (575) ("the public's eye" [481])—which Rousseau uses to describe both his sense of self in relation to others and the reception of his work—prefigures both the feared loss of authorial control and the growing cult of literary celebrity with which Romantic writers will contend. In his early life, Rousseau shows only abstract interest in the public; in fact, he uses the term "public" primarily to mean "the coterie." As his authorial presence grows, his imagined ideal audience seems ridiculously out of touch with the reality of his writings' reception. For example, Rousseau seems genuinely puzzled when the peasants he idealizes as pillars of value turn against him and collude with his detractors. But for a modern reader, Rousseau confirms what social historians such as George Rudé and E. P. Thompson note—namely, that popular culture, especially as influenced by public opinion, tends to be highly conservative. Despite a rebellious surface, the people usually identify with the status quo, a situation that works to Rousseau's disadvantage. Once he has angered those above him on the social ladder, their control over the organs of information—from publications to rumor and gossip—makes Rousseau a spectacle and allows him no self-defense. More important, the peasants have their own identification patterns and are more likely to equate their interests with the powerful than with a writer like Rousseau.

In response to feelings of being misunderstood or wronged, Rousseau blames

> nos sotes institutions civiles où le vrai bien public et la véritable justice sont toujours sacrifiés à je ne sais quel ordre apparent, destructif en effet de tout ordre, et qui ne fait qu'ajouter la sanction de l'autorité publique à l'oppression du foible et à l'iniquité du fort.   (327)

> our foolish civil institutions in which the true public good and genuine justice are always sacrificed to some apparent order or other, in fact destructive of all order, and which does nothing but add the sanction of public authority to the oppression of the weak and the iniquity of the strong.   (274)

When Rousseau expresses what we might now call paranoia—for example, when he is sure that "les planchers sous lesquels je suis ont des yeux" (279) ("the ceiling under which I live has eyes" [235]) or that "les espions m'obsédent" (325) ("spies plague me" [273])—he sounds like the main character in William Godwin's *Caleb Williams* (1794). Rousseau becomes obsessed with a world in which rumor and gossip predominate, newspapers and information are instrumentally controlled, and cabals and parties overwhelm those who care only for the "bien public" ("public good") and those who try to "dire ouvertement la vérité aux hommes" (223) ("tell the truth openly to men" [187]). In a paraphrase of Montaigne, but also in line with eighteenth-century attitudes, Rousseau calls public opinion "les jugemens insensés de la tourbe vulgaire des soi-disans grands et des soi-disans sages" (362) ("the senseless judgments of the vulgar mob of self-proclaimed grandees and self-proclaimed wise men" [304]). Opinion is a counterpoint to reason and based on incomplete information and irregular logic; public opinion, in Rousseau's world, is not critical debate and synthesis of ideas but an instrument of social control. Rousseau recognizes a public constrained by what William Blake, in *Songs of Experience*, would later call "mind-forg'd manacles" (27).

Rousseau knows that people want and need to be informed; in his youth he is a "nouvelliste" ("collector of news"). In retrospect, he ridicules his early interest, calling those who desire information "gobe-mouches" (184) ("crowd of gulls" [154]); later, he refers to public opinion as a "concours d'aboye-mens" (605) ("concurrence of carping" [507]) and sees the unanimity of the public voice as detrimental to the individual. Ironically, the more he tries to distance himself from the public, the more attention he arouses. By proclaiming himself an advocate of noble poverty and social freedom, he becomes a popular curiosity, as crowds of idle people visit and gawk (425 [357]). When opinion turns against him, however, particularly in the backlash against *Emile*, he eventually pays a high price for celebrity (573 [480]).

Book 12 of the *Confessions* enacts many of Rousseau's concerns about the public and reveals what were, for him, the worst qualities of a life often lived in the public eye. He experiences the lash of gossip and of public forums in which he is characterized as seditious; the clergy condemns his behavior, and governments legislate against him. Whenever he goes out, even on country roads in broad daylight, he finds himself publicly insulted, and he feels betrayed by the people he claims to defend (624 [523]). As the public's attitude toward him becomes increasingly hostile, he views the public as "esprits sans culture et sans lumiéres" (604) ("minds without cultivation and without enlightenment" [505]). He senses the collusion of public officials in making him reviled, and he calls the animosity toward him a public frenzy. Often recognized and persecuted as he travels, he chronicles "le spectacle de la haine du peuple" (636) ("the spectacle of the people's hatred" [532]) and feels like a "fugitif sur la terre" (594) ("fugitive on the earth" [497]). He describes being threatened with violence and pelted by muck as he walks on rural roads. Hooting and rock-throwing lead to more serious threats and finally to an attack on his house the night of the Môtiers fair in 1765. There is physical damage to the house during what can only be defined as a riot, but it is the psychological terror that lingers. As negative public opinion turns to violence against him, the gothic narration in book 12 culminates a lifetime of contradictory attitudes about the public and highlights the split between private and public self. The private Rousseau believes that truth can be found within and that language should express the soul. By contrast, the public world in which he must live demands deceit, just as it privileges outward appearances, the mundane, and traditional practices. In suggesting change, he becomes an enemy of the people.

Rousseau's narration in the *Confessions* often seems at odds with his social theorizing, which articulates a central Romantic paradox: the problematic relationship, as well as the varying goals and desires, of artist and individual, public and populace. The man who delineates the origins of inequality feels superior and claims that the public is dull and uninformed. He simultaneously aggrandizes the peasantry and despises the vulgar masses. He complains of oppression of the common people yet fears revolutionary action or any change in political hierarchy. In fact, while Rousseau argues in the *Lettre à d'Alembert sur les spectacles* that the rituals of public assembly can potentially secure good citizenship (*OC* 5: 114–15), he warns in *Du contrat social* that democracy is subject to private manipulation (3: 439 [4: 199]) and has a protean quality that makes it "sujet aux guerres civiles et aux agitations intestines" (3: 405) ("subject to civil wars and internal agitation" [4: 174]). His utopian sense of civic identification, celebrated during the early stages of the French Revolution, becomes equally a source of concern in movements toward unenlightened nationalism. Although the line of influence may not always be direct, the multiple ironies that permeate Rousseau's thought become the central irresolvable conundrums for Romanticism and prove an apt starting point for exploring the Romantic movement.

Sympathy and Sensibility in Rousseau's Sixth Walk and Wordsworth's "The Old Cumberland Beggar"

Lorraine J. Clark

William Hazlitt famously claimed that Rousseau and William Wordsworth "both create an interest out of nothing, or rather out of their own feelings . . . both wind their own being round whatever object occurs to them" (Howe 92). The "object" that the two authors "wind their own being round"—Rousseau in his prose reverie the Sixth Walk and Wordsworth in his poetic reverie "The Old Cumberland Beggar"—is not strictly speaking an object at all but a living, breathing human subject: a beggar whose destitute condition elicits or ought to elicit the speaker-observer's sympathy, compassion, and charity. Similar encounters with victims in distress—beggars, vagrants, prostitutes, bedlamites, Gypsies, impoverished old women—figure prominently in Romantic literature and especially the late-eighteenth-century literature of sensibility. In this respect, the chance meeting with a beggar in these two short works epitomizes the kind of situation that appears with variations in most of this literature and raises issues that are central to it.

"Sympathy," "sensibility," "compassion"—the terms represent the new ethos, which replaces rational judgment as the highest virtue. The moral character of the Man—and Woman—of Feeling is revealed to the extent that he or she does or does not commiserate with the victim in distress. Does the sight bring forth pity, contempt, ridicule and laughter, or abuse? It is interesting to realize how easily these responses can lapse into or be tainted by one another (Joseph Conrad would speak of "that form of contempt which is called pity" [174]) and how such responses—even the most benign—keep the victim at arm's length as "object." Spectatorial distance appears to be the very condition of sympathy.

What exactly are the dynamics of compassion as these two works reveal them to be? What are the relations among speaker-observer, beggar, nature, and human society? Which observer is more genuinely sympathetic: the Wordsworthian or the Rousseauian? Which one has more honesty, sincerity, or "authenticity"? Does the latter moral attribute displace sympathy to become the higher virtue? What kind of virtue *is* sympathy? Finally, is the spectatorial distance that seems to be the condition of sympathy for both writers the distance of the philosopher or of the poet? What, in other words, is the nature of reflection and its relation to sympathy as we see it in these two highly reflective meditations?

The context or setting of the encounters is a good point of departure for our own meditative ramble through these works and for a classroom discussion of the two authors. As Rousseau and Wordsworth, both solitary walkers, deliberately leave the precincts of society for those of nature, their thoughts revolve around the spectacle of a beggar they have come across. What makes the beggar an arresting object is surely not only his indigence but also an implicit recognition of a similarity of situation: he shares the alienated, marginal status of the poet-speakers, midway between nature and society. In him, they see themselves and ultimately the human condition, as they think, most clearly.

Poet-speakers and beggars rely on nature and society to exist and because of their dependence on society, may fear their uselessness. "But deem not this Man useless"—that is, do not banish him altogether from society—Wordsworth exhorts (line 67). The poem argues for a particular kind of moral usefulness such beggars in fact have for society, a usefulness that by analogy may defend the utility of the poet. Rousseau acknowledges his uselessness but carefully distinguishes it from moral turpitude and, like Wordsworth, proposes a different definition and defense of his own utility: "Leur tort n'a donc pas été de m'écarter de la societé comme un membre inutile, mais de m'en proscrire comme un membre pernicieux" (*Rêv.* 1059) ("Their wrong, then, was not to turn me out of society as a useless member, but to proscribe me from it as a pernicious member" [56]). Here too, the argument is that the poet-speaker, like the beggar, serves a useful moral function in society. Thus both these meditations may be in the end defenses of poetry and of the poetic imagination as the agent of a higher sympathy and utility.

Because of their powers of reflection and their relative affluence, our speakers are surely much further from raw nature and much closer to society than are the beggars; the difference in situation may bring "pity" nearer to "contempt." Wordsworth's beggar, barely human in his lack of consciousness, is a creature degraded almost to animal status, who might invite kicks rather than commiseration. In Wordsworth's poem "Gypsies," repugnance does replace compassion when the speaker complains that a group of Gypsies who remain in one spot during his twelve-hour walk are lazy and useless. To Wordsworth's charge, Coleridge snappishly replies that he was "overlooking the obvious truth that such repose might be as necessary for *them*, as a walk of the same continuance was pleasing or healthful for the more fortunate poet" (346; *Biographia*, ch. 22).

The slide from pity to contempt is much more explicitly acknowledged by Rousseau, who openly admits to his increasing suspicions that what he initially found to be amusing chatter on the part of the child-beggar was in fact a "harangue" in which the child had been carefully coached by his elders (1050 [49]). As always in Rousseau, the situation is more complex than it seems on the surface: it is not the child's degraded status that disgusts Rousseau but his likely corruption by society. The point remains, I think, that the easy descent from pity to contempt reveals a crack in the ideal of pity itself: perhaps it is only a concealed form of contempt, based on disguised inequality rather than on a compassionate equality of human nature. Wordsworth calls himself, as a poet, "a man speaking to men," differing in degree but not in kind (Preface to the *Lyrical Ballads*). But is he? Is Rousseau? Isn't the concern that both speakers have for the beggars the highly reflective sympathy of the civilized and socialized imagination, rather than the instinctual, spontaneous sympathy that Rousseau claims in the second *Discours* characterizes humanity in the state of nature? Isn't such sympathy, then, not egalitarian but elitist?

The real obstacle to natural sympathy for Rousseau, however, is not his superior social status as gentleman walker and his highly developed capacity for reflection but the "contract" that inevitably becomes established through habitual encounters with the beggar. The nature of this contract and its implications for sympathy and the larger question of moral virtue is the real center of both Rousseau's Walk and Wordsworth's poem. What effect does the "contract," or tacit understanding inevitably arising between benefactor and beneficiary, have on our speakers' compassion? What are the implications for their virtue?

As Rousseau describes this contract (1054 [52]), repeated acts of charity engender an expectation of their indefinite continuance that clearly destroys the possibility of genuine, spontaneous, freely given alms. It alienates duty from inclination to the point that, even if the obligation concurred with his desires, it is enough to kill those desires (1053 [51]). And thus society perverts our natural tendencies, even beneficence (1052 [50]).

For Wordsworth, by contrast, the contract established between society and the beggar—benefactor and beneficiary—consolidates and reinforces natural compassion:

> Where'er the aged Beggar takes his rounds,
> The mild necessity of use compels
> To acts of love; and habit does the work
> Of reason; yet prepares that after-joy
> Which reason cherishes. And thus the soul,
> By that sweet taste of pleasure unpursued,
> Doth find herself insensibly disposed
> To virtue and true goodness. . . .   (98–105)

Wordsworth sees no conflict between inclination and duty, or between natural and societal compassion. For Wordworth, what Rousseau sees as "chains" of obligation strengthen—rather than pervert—natural sympathy. Further, in Wordsworth's account, virtue does not consist in subordinating one's inclinations to one's duties. Nor does the fact that virtue becomes the automatic, unthinking, involuntary exercise of compassion (through charity)—instead of a free and conscious choice—mitigate in any way its morality.

Nor, finally, does the ultimate self-interestedness of this compassion qualify its virtue. What is it that really motivates Wordsworth's villagers to perform their compassionate acts of charity? Two things: self-gratification and their reward in heaven. Wordsworth's beggar is useful because

> . . . —all behold in him
> A silent monitor, which on their minds
> Must needs impress a transitory thought
> Of self-congratulation, to the heart
> Of each recalling his peculiar boons (122–26)

The villagers are like the speaker's neighbor, who "builds her hope in heaven" (161). For Rousseau, such charity would surely be compromised, if not entirely perverted, by the fact that it has become mere obligation and necessity, not freely given, and that it is motivated almost entirely by self-interest. Further, this alleged virtue—because it has not involved any conflict between inclination and duty and hence none of the voluntary sacrifice of desire to duty—does not constitute true virtue. His own inability to sacrifice desire to duty is, he admits, what makes him convinced he is not "virtuous" (1052–53 [51]). The virtue of Wordsworth's villagers is, for Rousseau, clearly no virtue at all.

Rousseau does appeal, however, to a higher morality and a higher sympathy of "inaction," and it is here that the juxtaposition with Wordsworth has its most striking implications. For Rousseau appeals to what is surely the higher sympathy—and morality—of the Romantic, poetic imagination and thus provides a defense of poetry (and specifically of Romantic poetry) superior to that supplied by perhaps its greatest apologist, Wordsworth himself: "Tant que j'agis librement je suis bon et je ne fais que du bien; mais sitôt que je sens le joug, soit de la nécessité soit des hommes je deviens rebelle ou plustot rétif, alors je suis nul" (1059) ("As long as I act freely, I am good and do only good," he insists, "but as soon as I feel the yoke either of necessity or of men, I become rebellious, or rather, recalcitrant; then I am ineffectual" [56]). In order to be "effectual"—that is, useful—he chooses not to act at all (1051 [50]). Only thus can he remain uncompromised and truly free: "Je n'ai jamais cru que la liberté de l'homme consistat à faire ce qu'il veut, mais bien à ne jamais faire ce qu'il ne veut pas" (1059) ("I have never believed that man's freedom consists in doing what he wants, but rather in never doing what he does not want to do" [56]).

Rousseau's honest self-acknowledgment is one Wordsworth never makes; idealizing his "sympathetic" relations with poor and rural humanity, he sees himself always as "a man among men"—despite remaining, as Coleridge again so astutely observed, a "spectator *ab extra*." One might conclude that his aloofness puts Rousseau in the position of the "pitiless" philosopher he describes in the second *Discours*: "C'est la Philosophie qui l'isole; c'est par elle qu'il dit en secret, à l'aspect d'un homme souffrant, peris si tu veux, je suis en sureté" (3: 156) ("Philosophy isolates him; because of it he says in secret, at the sight of a suffering man: perish if you will, I am safe" [3: 37]). Rousseau's explicit—and Wordsworth's denied but implicit—freedom from action and involvement is summarized by Rousseau's new metaphor, not that of the cold philosopher or even the solitary walker, but that of a spectator watching a play: "Ils ne me sont même indifferens qu'en ce qui se rapporte à moi; car dans leurs rapports entre eux, ils peuvent encor m'interesser et m'émouvoir comme les personnages d'un Drame que je verrois répresenter" (1057) ("I am not really indifferent about them [humanity], except in what relates to me; for in their relations among themselves, they can still concern and move me as would the characters in a Drama I might see performed" [54]). Removed from the chains of obligation that pervert spontaneous sympathy, Rousseau— through his sympathetic, Romantic imagination—can enter freely into the lives of others, with an acknowledged spectatorial distance that he, unlike Wordsworth, fully realizes is the very condition of his sympathy. Is this attitude coldly selfish and irresponsible? Perhaps. But we should also consider what comes out of this apparently "useless" stance: the freely given, spontaneously charitable gift of Rousseau's own reflective poetry of sensibility.

From the Solitary Walker to the *Flâneur*: Baudelaire's Caricature of Rousseau

Jean Starobinski

Charles Baudelaire did not like Rousseau. He had read him with enough attention, however, not to remain indifferent and not to cling to hostility on principle, as he did toward Voltaire, the antipoet. In Baudelaire's critical texts, in his intimate journals, and in *Spleen de Paris*, Rousseau was both a model and an adversary. For a time, Baudelaire imagined giving the collection of his prose poems a Rousseauian title: *Le Promeneur solitaire*. He noted on a list of possible projects: "On Jean-Jacques—sentimental and vile author" (2: 54; "De quelques préjugés contemporains"). The avowed Rousseauism of George Sand definitively situated Rousseau among those who, refusing to believe in hell and sin, placed undue confidence in nature and in their own feelings. Jean-Jacques, who "got high without hashish," had "a superlative idea of his own moral value" (Baudelaire, "Le Poème du haschich" [1: 436; *Les Paradis artificiels*, sec. 4]). He deified himself. Baudelaire's criticism was that Rousseau confused imagining virtue, having a sensation of moral goodness, with possessing a true "practical aptitude for virtue." In other words, his criticism targeted the confusion between aesthetics and ethics in Rousseau:

> He completely confuses dreams with actions, and his imagination, over-heated by the enchanting spectacle of his own mended and idealized nature, substitutes that fascinating image of himself for the real individual he is, so poor in will, so rich in vanity. As a result, he ends up decreeing his apotheosis in the clear and simple terms that, for him, contain a whole world of abominable pleasures: *"I am the most virtuous of men!"*
>
> (1: 436)

Baudelaire develops this critique of Rousseau in narrative form in his prose poem "Le Gâteau" (1861), where we discover a peculiar, perhaps semi-conscious strategy. Baudelaire echoes two famous passages from Rousseau, reworking and reinterpreting the motifs, which are easily recognizable: the exalting ascension to the mountains (*La Nouvelle Héloïse*, pt. 1, ch. 23) and the peasants' battle (*Rêv.*, Ninth Walk, which served as the starting point for the present study). Baudelaire thus rereads Rousseau in order to refute him with his own images. He readjusts two scenes to make them say the opposite of what Rousseau wished to lead his readers to concede.

In the first part of "Le Gâteau," in which, no doubt, a personal memory of Baudelaire's intrudes—a trip Baudelaire took to the Pyrenees in 1838 in the company of his father-in-law—readers have noted how close the expressions of happiness are to those found in the famous letter by Saint-Preux, Julie's lover, on Valais (Kopp; Gutwirth). In this case, the fiction uses a mixture of youthful reminiscences and literary formulas: "I stood in the middle of a land-scape of irresistible grandeur and nobility" (Baudelaire 1: 297). Human activity is announced only by "the bells of the cattle grazing out of sight, far away, on the other side of another mountain." But the description of the harmonious countryside, which forms the first part of the narrative, is soon jarred by the dissonance of irony. The passage makes clear, now, that the narrator is making fun of himself: his feelings have steered him wrong. The ecstasy of fusion is devalued almost as soon as it is evoked: "In short, owing to the beauty that surrounded me and filled me with enthusiasm, I felt at perfect peace with myself and with the universe; I even believe that, in my perfect bliss and my total obliviousness to all earthly evil, I had reached the point of no longer finding so ridiculous the newspapers that claim man is born good" (297–98). The legitimacy of the word "perfect," repeated with insistence, is called into question by that very insistence, and thus becomes suspect. As it is used here, the modifier is more appropriate for describing the effect of a euphoria des-tined to disappear quickly.

"Man is born good" is a statement Rousseau asserted many times in the *Discours sur l'origine et les fondements de l'inégalité*, the *Profession de foi du vicaire savoyard*, the *Lettre à Christophe de Beaumont*, the third *Dialogue*, and elsewhere. At the end of the sentence from "Le Gâteau," Rousseau's words mark the ironic disavowal of the ecstatic impulse. Rousseau is not named: his thinking is attacked in the vulgar form it assumes in "the news-papers" that extol the virtues of optimism and progress. Like Joseph de Maistre before him, Baudelaire isolates the celebrated formulation of Rous-seau's doctrine, which, rejecting traditional theology, denies original sin and its propagation from one generation to the next. Rousseau dared maintain that vice is external in origin and that sin is not part of human nature: therein lies Baudelaire's grievance. We immediately understand that, for the narrator of the prose poem, the journalistic diffusion of the idea of natural goodness disqualifies it: it has lost all philosophical authority and has become part of some impersonal humanitarian chatter.

In *La Nouvelle Héloïse*, Rousseau's hero describes the joy and purifying relief he experienced as he climbed the peaks: the traveler was freed from evil in leaving the cities below, where men, captive to appearance and *amour-propre*, suffer the constraints of poverty and inequality. Saint-Preux discovers a world both sublime and pastoral, living closer to primitive equity and ex-periencing the joys of "disinterested humanity" and "the zeal for hospitality." In Rousseau's text, the social idyll adds to the aesthetic delight of contem-plating vast horizons (*OC* 2: 79–80 [*CW* 6: 65]). The mountain village is the place of the gift. Nothing is asked of the traveler; on the contrary, he is offered everything he might desire. Surrounded by the eagerness of his hosts, Saint-Preux tastes the hospitality received and becomes the center of a happy world, just as in the Ninth Walk. There, Rousseau becomes the center of a fete in which "contented faces" respond to his equitable distribution of a little treat.

In La Chevrette (*Rêv.* 1092–93 [83–84]), Rousseau does not consider his act true alms but sees it merely as a better "amusement" (compared to that of good society), a little "comedy" whose "denouement" he was happy to provide. In carefully rereading Rousseau's text, we find that the equitable distribution of the apples is an aesthetic choice, even though it is determined by an ethical condemnation of the violence provoked by the gingerbread thrown this way and that. And in this aesthetic choice, the narcissistic component, as Rousseau himself admits, is very important.

Baudelaire cannot accept any of that: not the way Rousseau asks nature to guarantee both the beauty of the world and the goodness of humankind; not the way a little gift exhibited in front of witnesses permits Rousseau to acquit himself of the charges he makes against "good society"; not the way Rousseau undertakes to find, in the resources of his own conscience—in his unfailing innnocence—the compensation for the evils society has made him suffer. Above all, Baudelaire does not accept the idealized image of a mountain society in which a virtuous autarky ensures both frugality and abundance.

Rousseau proposed the little comedy in two acts, in which the scene of true joy follows the scene of violence and of "gouts exclusifs engendrés par le mépris" (*Rêv.* 1093) ("exclusive tastes engendered by scorn" [84]). In constructing his own diptych, in "Le Gâteau," Baudelaire reverses the two scenes. The bright scene is the first one described, but it is checked by irony, since, at the ethical level, this country nobility (with its premonitory counterpoint of white and black) is stripped of any convincing value. The dark scene follows, and violence is irrevocable. The curtain falls; the final dot is set in place at the moment when the work of destruction leaves no room for hope. Thus Baudelaire uses Rousseauian elements to change the order that allowed Rousseau to repair the damage done and that permitted redemption to triumph over evil. The critique functions by inverting the consoling sequence of events. In Rousseau, the fete follows the brawl; in Baudelaire, the brawl follows "virtuistic" ecstasy.

How does Baudelaire construct the scene of evil after his flight into pseudounity with the surroundings? The narration calls attention to anything that might contradict the obliviousness to "earthly evil" (297) and the flight to false ideas. Heaviness, "the imperative of incurable matter" (298) can be felt in the very body of the narrator, who has taken pleasure in his disincarnated "lightness" (of his own thoughts, of the surrounding atmosphere [297]). Artifice and commerce intrude: Where is natural purity when the traveler decides to mix "a certain elixir" sold by "the pharmacists" into the melted snow? He then pulls from his pocket "a big piece of bread":

> I was calmly cutting up my bread when a very soft noise made me look
> up. Before me stood a ragged creature, black and tousled, whose hollow,

fierce and, as it were, supplicating eyes were devouring the piece of bread. And I heard him sigh, in a low and raucous voice, the word "cake"! I could not keep myself from laughing upon hearing the name with which he had wished to honor my bread, which was nearly white, and I cut off a nice slice and offered it to him.   (298)

The "soft noise" destroys the magic established by the immense and fragile silence of the beginning. The child who has just received the slice of bread is immediately "knocked over by another little savage, come from who knows where, and so perfectly similar to the first that he might have been taken for his twin. Together they rolled about on the ground, fighting for the precious prey, neither wishing to sacrifice half to his brother" (298). After a lengthy and atrocious struggle, there is no longer "any object of the battle: the *piece of bread* had disappeared, scattered into crumbs like the *grains of sand* with which it was now mixed" (299; my emphasis). The annihilation of the "object of the battle" recalls the scene in La Chevrette, in which young people maim one another "brutalement, pour s'arracher avidement quelques *morceaux de pain d'epice* foulés aux pieds et couverts de *boue*" (*Rêv* 1093; my emphasis) ("brutally . . . to grab avidly at some *pieces of gingerbread* trampled underfoot and covered with *mud*" [84]). In returning to sand or mud, the gift of food is no longer fit for consumption: the effect of the gift is disastrous and may even be attributed to a perverse intention. We also note that, in Rousseau, the debasing hyperbole of "troupeaux d'hommes avilis par la misére" (1093) ("*herds* of men degraded by abject poverty" [84; my emphasis]) finds its counterpart in the Baudelairean expression "little *savage*" (in his writings, Rousseau gives an idyllic sense to "savage").

Let us note, in addition, that Baudelaire, as in many other texts, adopts here an allegorical view. The first receiver of the slice of bread necessarily has only one rival, and that rival has to look like him. Not Cain and Abel, but two Cains, who are equally mean. As a result, the combat, which takes on an emblematic value, becomes a lesson concerning human nature under conditions of poverty. The narrator is now a dismayed spectator who can no longer return to his initial ecstasy of contemplating the landscape. Rousseau, in contrast, remains a participant in the two scenes (a contributor to them); he sets them against each other, tallies up the two events, and—weighing the value given and the pleasure taken—draws up the balance sheet to his advantage:

Je sentois avec satisfaction la différence qu'il y a des gouts sains et des plaisirs naturels à ceux que fait naitre l'oppulence et qui ne sont guéres que des plaisirs de moquerie et des gouts exclusifs engendrés par le mépris.   (1093)

I felt with satisfaction the difference that separates healthy tastes and natural pleasures from those which opulence engenders and which are hardly anything but pleasures of mockery and exclusive tastes engendered by scorn.   (84)

In Baudelaire's prose poem, the narrator does not attribute any merit to himself. Has he performed an act of charity? He sees the first child, meets his imploring gaze, registers his envy, and laughs at the only word pronounced: "cake." A disproportionate, inappropriate word. Then he cuts off a slice of bread and offers it. No mention of compassion. And, when the second child makes his brutal appearance, the narrator does not attempt to intervene in the struggle. No additional alms, no intercession. The accumulated details lead us to suppose that he is fascinated and paralyzed by the spectacle of evil. (Curiosity about evil is never absent in Baudelaire, and often—particularly in the narrative "La Fausse Monnaie" [1: 323–24]—it appears more excusable to him than hypocritical fraud and simulated goodness.) The description is both comic and repugnant. For it records at great length the vicissitudes of a struggle between equals that succeeds only in destroying the coveted object. Every part of the body parades by: hair, ears, eyes, teeth, claws, neck, stomach. The narrator has taken pains to vary the aspects of the battle, while using paraleipsis to suggest that he is reporting only a small part of it: "What is the point of describing?" (298), he asks, having just depicted a series of incidents and provisional triumphs.

In fact, Baudelaire constructed his narrative with an obvious concern for visual effect and with faithfulness to a "dream": his entire aesthetics can be recognized here. The bitten ear and "the bloody bite" spit out by one of the fighters increase the precision of the scene and give a splash of color to a text whose chromatic values of bright and dark have been those of a drawing or an engraving. Several terms used in the bright part of the prose poem and repeated in the dark section make the reversal all the more troubling. The word "perfect," used earlier to modify the narrator's "peace" and "bliss" in experiencing the beauty of the world, now intensifies the violence: "a perfectly fratricidal war" (299). The "total obliviousness to all earthly evil" elicits a joy that has "totally disappeared" (299) by the end. Not even the journey of an (at first) happy consciousness ("I was traveling" [297]) is spared an absurd, mechanical, and degraded repetition, when the coveted object "travels" (298) from hand to hand and from pocket to pocket.

Two "little men" and a disputed slice of bread are all that is needed for the scene to be turned upside down, transforming a subjective peace into the most objective of wars. Another symmetry is also striking: just as the first part gives an unwarranted ethical meaning to the beauty of the landscape, the second part attributes an unwarranted aesthetic value to certain aspects of the "hideous struggle." Note that the "superb curse in patois" (298) presupposes an ironic detachment and an attention to proper usage that might appear displaced, were we not aware that Baudelaire has become an accomplice (that is, he pretends to be an accomplice) of the literate reader: the narrative appeared in the periodical *La Presse* (24 Sept. 1862). The irony expressed in relation to the newspapers that "claim man is born good" suggests that Baudelaire knows the stylistic means to reach a newspaper-reading public (which harbors scorn for those who prefer another newspaper). The mixture of the beautiful and the ugly is deeply distressing. The prose poem, which closes with a sentence the narrator repeats "endlessly," thus leaves the reader no possibility of resting easy:

> This spectacle had clouded over the landscape for me, and the calm joy my soul had taken pleasure in [*s'ébaudissait*] before seeing these little men had totally disappeared; I remained sad for quite a long time, endlessly repeating: "There is thus a superb country where bread is called cake, and where it is a treat so rare that it is enough to engender a perfectly fratricidal war."   (299)

The concluding meditation makes sadness and opacity fall on the landscape. The "calm joy" of the beginning cannot withstand a reality test. In the retrospective evocation of that joy, the bawdy expression *s'ébaudissait* introduces, once more, an ironic and diminutive value. Joy has lost its universal dimension. Mystical unity, sensed a moment earlier, has been reduced to a little personal titillation. The transparence so dear to Rousseau is done for. The view of a ruthless struggle of "little men" contradicts the idea of childhood innocence and original goodness. An offered slice of bread has become a casus belli for its beneficiaries, each of whom is incapable of "sacrific[ing] half for his brother" (298). In the final reflection, the social dimension of evil appears fully, and we are not astonished to find in Baudelaire's writing an indictment— with political overtones—of the "superb country where bread is called cake." But contrary to Rousseau, Baudelaire does not radically distinguish between human nature and social evil. For him, evil is a fundamental anthropological given, not the consequence of a defect in the formulation of rules of civil association.

NOTE

This essay is drawn from Jean Starobinski, *Largesse*, trans. Jane Marie Todd (Chicago: U of Chicago P, 1997), 120–27. Used with permission from the University of Chicago Press.

Altered States

Marie-Hélène Huet

In the brief text he wrote on the two hundred fiftieth anniversary of the birth of Jean-Jacques Rousseau and published a year later, Claude Lévi-Strauss described what he saw as the most constant and unifying paradox of the philosopher's work:

> that Rousseau could have, simultaneously, advocated the study of the most remote men, while [having] mostly given himself to the study of that particular man who seems the closest—himself; and secondly that, throughout his work, the systematic will to identify with the other goes hand in hand with an obstinate refusal to identify with the self. (35)

For Lévi-Strauss, Rousseau was the first thinker to assert that in a corrupt society governed by self-love, one could reclaim one's humanity only by losing the sense of one's individuality in a primitive identification with humankind and with all forms of life. Lévi-Strauss quoted two passages from the *Rêveries* as examples of the privileged moments in which the individual achieves an epiphanic connection to a point *"beyond* man with all that is alive and, consequently, suffers" (40). The first example is taken from the Second Walk, where Rousseau describes his feelings as he regained consciousness after being knocked down by a dog: "je n'avois nulle notion distincte de mon individu. . . . je sentois dans tout mon être un calme ravissant auquel chaque fois que je me le rappelle je ne trouve rien de comparable dans toute l'activité des plaisirs connus" (1005) ("I had no distinct notion of my person. . . . I felt a rapturous calm in my whole being; and each time I remember it, I find nothing comparable to it in all the activity of known pleasures [12]). In the Seventh Walk, Rousseau describes again the unique experience of thoroughly losing the awareness of the self as separate identity: "Je sens des extases, des ravissements inexprimables à me fondre pour ainsi dire dans le systême des êtres, à m'identifier avec la nature entiére" (1065–66) ("I feel ecstasies and inexpressible raptures in blending, so to speak, into the system of beings and in making myself one with the whole of nature" [61]).

This primitive, fundamental capacity to erase, even briefly, the sense of self results from pity. As Rousseau notes in the *Discours sur l'origine et les fondements de l'inégalité*, pity, one of only two faculties that precede reason in the natural human being, allows us to identify closely with a suffering other; it mitigates the love of self that impels our instinct toward self-preservation; it ensures a moderation that, in turn, furthers the survival of the species. More important for Lévi-Strauss, through pity "man begins by experiencing himself as identical to all his fellows. And he will never forget this primitive experience" (38).

The second element of the paradox consists in Rousseau's denial of a comfortable, self-proclaimed identity, "a refusal of all that can make the self 'acceptable' . . . in truth, I am not 'me,' but the weakest, the most humble of 'others.' Such is the discovery of the *Confessions*" (39). Although Lévi-Strauss does not examine, in this text, the tensions between pity (as the feeling that moves us toward the other) and the preservation instinct entirely focused on the self, his interpetation of pity gives it a pride of place, a preeminence that undermines any desire—even in the least sociable of philosophers—to develop a sense of self completely separated from social exchanges or divorced from the primordial awareness that one first feels *like another*.

A few years before Lévi-Strauss's homage to Rousseau, Jacques Derrida speculated that pity is, in fact, not a primordial faculty but rather a derivation of the love of self. In *Of Grammatology* he noted that pity "is *almost* primitive. . . . it is less an estrangement and an interruption of the love of self than its first and most necessary consequence." Derrida founded his assertion partly on a passage from *Emile* in which Rousseau writes that "the child's first sentiment is love of self [*l'amour de soi*]; and his second, which is derived from it, is love of those about him." Without engaging in the controversy that prompted Derrida's reading (an argument over the origin of languages), we can observe that, in *Emile*, Rousseau speaks specifically of a child's "love of those around him" (Derrida 174) and that this feeling is not pity and cannot be confused with it. For pity is not love, but a more fundamental capacity to lose one's sense of self in the other's suffering. Nonetheless, both Lévi-Strauss and Derrida, in spite of their diverging interpretations of the definition and role of pity, emphasize the complexity of the opposite dynamic of love of self and pity: the first of these original faculties always privileges survival and self-preservation; the second always moves the subject toward the other.

The *Rêveries* has long been considered Rousseau's culminating moment of self-pity. As he feels betrayed and persecuted in human society, he falls back on himself, in wonderment at his lasting ability to suffer among others and because of them. What do we learn from Rousseau's ultimate meditations on the status of the individual in society? For Rousseau, the *Rêveries* points essentially to a return to a love of the self strengthened by pity—that is, a love of the self rendered even more forceful by pity's capacity to feel the other's suffering. That is, should we consider the *Rêveries* as the last avatar of pity, a text in which Rousseau's natural disposition to identify with the other's sorrow is reinvested in his afflicted self?

In the Third Walk, Rousseau traces his rejection of society to the start of his work on *La Profession de foi du vicaire savoyard*, included in *Emile*. During the last years of his life, Rousseau delights in his fully reclaimed solitude: "Réduit à moi seul, je me nourris il est vrai de ma propre substance mais elle ne s'épuise pas et je me suffis à moi-même" (1075) ("Left only to myself, I feed, it is true, on my own substance; but it is not depleted. And I am sufficient unto myself" [70]). Logically, perhaps, this deliberate estrangement from society also seems to signal a dulling of Rousseau's sense of pity.

Rousseau explains, in the Sixth Walk, why he eventually decides to avoid a young crippled boy who begs near the Enfer tollgate exit. The pleasure to give, he realizes, has become an unbearable form of duty. Rousseau's natural capacity to feel pity (1053 [51]), or to yield to a feeling of pity, is dead. In the past, Rousseau underlines, he experienced pity so intensely that it dominated all other desires, including his personal interests. Pity was so strong a feeling, indeed a passion, that it vanquished reason and perhaps even duty.

The constraint Rousseau experiences when giving in to pity has shattered his desired isolation by introducing a form of social contract that he can no longer abide: "Je sais qu'il y a une espéce de contrat et même le plus saint de tous entre le bienfaiteur et l'obligé. C'est une sorte de societé qu'ils forment l'un avec l'autre, plus étroite que celle qui unit les hommes en général" (1053) ("I know that there is a kind of contract, and even the holiest of all, between the benefactor and the beneficiary. They form a sort of society with each other, more restricted than the one which unites men in general" [52]). These lines eloquently disclose what Rousseau has only suggested previously: that if pity, by turning us toward the other, makes it possible for us to become sociable, it also allows for a corruption of the natural state by producing unbearable restrictions—so much so that pity contains the germs of its own destruction: "je me suis souvent abstenu d'une bonne œuvre que j'avois le desir et le pouvoir de faire, effrayé de l'assujetissement auquel dans la suite je m'allois soumettre si je m'y livrois inconsidérément" (1054) ("I have often abstained from a good action I had the desire and the power to do, frightened of the subjection I would submit myself to afterward if I yielded to it without reflection" [52]). Far from experiencing pity as a primitive identity that, temporarily at least, puts the other before the self, Rousseau now feels subjected to a sense of duty that disfigures pity's pure, natural, selfless drive.

In describing the transformation of pity into moral duty as a natural effect of the relationship between giver and receiver, Rousseau notes:

> quand je fais un don c'est un plaisir que je me donne. Or le plaisir de remplir ses devoirs est de ceux que la seule habitude de la vertu fait naître: ceux qui nous viennent immédiatement de la nature ne s'élévent pas si haut que cela.

> when I give a gift, it is a pleasure I give myself. Now, the pleasure of fulfilling our duties is one of those that only the habit of virtue engenders; those which come to us immediately from nature do not rise so high.

Rousseau dates the changes he has suffered from the moment when society made him forsake his instinct to feel pity—that is, "aussitot que mes malheurs ont commencé" (1054) ("as soon as my misfortunes began" [52]). He continues: "mes propres sentimens pour les autres ont souffert des changmens que j'ai trouvé dans les leurs. . . . comment pourrai-je garder les mêmes sentimens pour ceux en qui je trouve le contraire de ce qui les fit naitre? (1054–55) ("with the change in the feelings of others toward me came a change in my own feelings toward them. . . . how could I keep the same feelings for those in whom I find the opposite of what engendered those feelings?" [52–53]). In this light, the most serious part of Rousseau's misfortunes may be none other than the loss of the spontaneous impulse that allowed him to feel another being's unhappiness and to yield to the natural desire to help.

In a key sentence resuming his current predicament, Rousseau writes, "Quel naturel resisteroit sans s'altérer à une situation pareille à la mienne?" (1055) ("What natural temperament could resist a situation similar to mine without being altered?" [53]). No doubt, we should give these words their strongest meaning. The specificity of Rousseau's forced isolation and his many sorrows have destroyed his ability to feel the primitive impulse of pity and have altered the Glaucus-like remnants of natural humankind that, disfigured but still standing, had presided over the philosopher's investigation of the individual's original state. As a result, Rousseau has become "null" (the word is reiterated in the Sixth Walk). In the First Walk he has already declared, "je suis nul desormais parmi les hommes, et c'est tout ce que je puis être n'ayant plus avec eux de rélation reelle, de véritable societé. . . . m'abstenir est devenu mon unique devoir" (1000) ("I am henceforth null among men, and that is all I can be, no longer having any real relations or genuine society with them" [7; trans. modified]). He repeats the idea in the Sixth Walk: "[L'adversité] dont je suis la proye . . . ne m'a rendu que nul" (1055–56). The translators, perplexed perhaps by this odd formulation, proposed a slightly altered sentence: "[The adversity] to which I am prey . . . has only made me ineffectual" (53). Considering the formulation "Ne m'a rendu que nul"—literally, "has made me only null"—we have to wonder how the absolute concept of "null" can be restricted in this way. Certainly this modification initially underlines the fact that abstention is an alternative to revenge. The alternative would be marked by an apparently more absolute negative: to wrong another would be *not* just, *not* virtuous, contrary to what Rousseau perceives as his good nature. By contrast, in one who has been egregiously wronged by society, being simply *null* may be an expression of moderation.

Such a reading, however, simplifies the changed relationship between Rousseau and society. Estrangement is not simply isolation. Self-pity is not just the disfiguration of an initial capacity to feel like a suffering other. Rather, abstention from doing good, from repeating an initial charitable gift, produces the sense of negative freedom that alone can liberate the doer from a contractual obligation. Rousseau expands: "Je m'abstiens d'agir: car toute ma foiblesse est pour l'action, toute ma force est négative" (1059) ("I abstain from acting, for all my weakness is with regard to action, all my strength is negative" [56]). In the First Walk, Rousseau has noted, "Les particuliers meurent, mais les corps collectifs ne meurent point" (998) ("Individuals die, but not collective groups" [6]). Even as he proclaims his solitude—the often-quoted "Je n'ai plus en ce monde ni prochain, ni semblables, ni fréres" (999) ("I no longer have neighbors, fellow creatures, or brothers in this world" [6])—Rousseau is forced to acknowledge the collective passions that survive the individual's (in)capacity to enter the social contract. Moreover, we can read in these lines another echo of the conflict between the general will, which cannot err, and the individual interests that, in the collective body, negate each other. Rousseau has said in the *Contrat social* (book 2, ch. 3) that, just as individuals die, individual wills destroy each other. In the *Rêveries*, Rousseau proclaims himself a unique individual, mortal but rightful. The collective body of Rousseau's persecutors may have erred; in doing so, however, society has also liberated Rousseau, in a negative but no less profound manner.

At this point, the reciprocity that characterizes any legitimate contract, be it political, social, or personal, is no longer possible: "j'ai perdu pour jamais l'idée de ramener de mon vivant le public sur mon compte, et même ce retour ne pouvant plus être reciproque me seroit desormais bien inutile" (997–98) ("I gave up for ever the idea of winning the public back over to my side during my lifetime; and, for that matter, now that this winning them back can no longer be reciprocal, it would henceforth be quite useless to me" [5]). Indeed, we can read the *Rêveries* as the proclamation of a freedom as great, in its negativity, as the primitive self-reliance that made the other's help unnecessary for the natural individual. Rousseau may now claim a regained autonomy ("je me suffis à moi-même" [1075] ["I am sufficient unto myself" (70)]).

The *promeneur* walks back toward the lost natural state, divesting himself, in the process, of the *amour-propre* that resulted from the first social interactions. In the second *Discours*, Rousseau forcefully describes the birth of this fateful passion:

> Chacun commença à regarder les autres et à vouloir être regardé soi-même, et l'estime publique eut un prix. . . . la fermentation causée par ces nouveaux levains produisit enfin des composés funestes au bonheur et à l'innocence.   (3: 169–70)

> Each one began to look at the others and to want to be looked at himself, and public esteem had a value. . . . the fermentation caused by these new leavens eventually produced compounds fatal to happiness and innocence.   (3: 47)

The Eighth Walk makes it clear: "Je n'eus jamais beaucoup de pente à l'amour propre, mais cette passion factice s'étoit exaltée en moi dans le monde" ("I never had much of a bent for amour-propre, but this factitious passion had become magnified in me when I was in the social world"). But now, "redevenant amour de moi même il est rentré dans l'ordre de la nature et m'a délivré du joug de l'opinion" (1079) ("again becoming love of myself, it returned to the natural order and delivered me of the yoke of opinion" [73]).

The *Rêveries* thus adds a dimension to Rousseau's long meditation on the troubled relationship between the individual and a society by no means prepared by nature but still made possible by pity. In this last reflection, Rousseau reclaims one of humankind's natural drives—the love of the self—while acknowledging the loss of the other natural drive—the feeling of pity. The ecstatic moments Lévi-Strauss quotes, in which Rousseau seems to lose himself in communion with nature, are not the natural effects of pity; they do not move him toward other people but away from them. Indeed, it is when the effects of society lessen that Rousseau can claim that "je redeviens ce que la nature a voulu" (1084; Eighth Walk) ("I again become what nature wanted" [76]). Yet, as Rousseau knows better than anyone else, there is no possible return to the original state of nature and no regaining of the perfect balance between love of self and pity. Rather, Rousseau's last achievement lies in having attained another mental state—altered, but no less exhilarating: when the love of self is no longer moderated by the opposite movement of pity, Rousseau at last can feel liberated from any impulsive move toward the other. This negative freedom has a price, no doubt. Rousseau has forsaken the pleasure of doing good, but abstention from action—"le seul bien qui soit desormais en ma puissance" (1051; Sixth Walk) ("the only good which might henceforth be within my power" [50])—has produced a unique form of sovereignty over the subject, which may ultimately be the only form of absolute freedom left.

Rêveries of Idleness

Pierre Saint-Amand

The history of the Age of Reason's "Great Confinement" does not concern madness alone. In his *Madness and Civilization* (*Histoire de la folie*), Michel Foucault has convincingly shown that the institutions of the absolute monarchy engaged, as well, in a concerted attempt to forbid laziness. Supported by a transcendent ethics, the implacable law of labor resists the slothful. Because the slothful exists outside the new bourgeois order, outside the world of production and commerce, it must be eradicated. The threat of imprisonment sends the unemployed back to work, where they are busied with "the endless leisure of a labor without utility or profit" and immediately subjugated to the new administration of the state (57).

In *Discipline and Punish* (*Surveiller et punir*), Foucault—delving even further into the repression of the slothful—analyzes the refusal to work as an offense committed against the useful and productive human body. Instead of being a simple archaeology of work, *Discipline and Punish*, with its genealogical perspective on the operation of power, examines the dialectic between work and sloth and its immanence in the affairs of state. What Foucault calls the "political technology of the body" (26) refers to the way in which the body is invested with power, the way in which it is marked, constructed, and assigned the role of signifier—in other words, the way in which the body is subjugated and placed in a political field. This technology of the body is based, above all, on the mechanisms of production: the most useful body is that of the worker, plugged into the machinery of production; its menacing other is the body of a lazy individual, in disharmony with norms of utility.

In the repertory of eighteenth-century punishments, work was conceived of as a penalty intended to combat laziness and vagrancy. The way to correct an offense against usefulness was to impose a change of attitude; imprisoning the lazy was a means of promoting work. Forced labor was considered to be a cure for the lazy, who would internalize an outlook based on economic reconstruction and personal reform. Foucault quotes a reformist legislator of the period: "The man who does not find his subsistence must be made to desire to procure it for himself by work; he is offered it by supervision and discipline; in a sense he is forced to acquire it, and he is then tempted by the bait of gain" (*Discipline* 122).

Standing outside society's economic order, the slothful individual is thus dangerous. He does not conform to the socioeconomic contract, nor does he participate in the public performance of work that defines the citizen. Work, then, can be thought of as the central resource of the new disciplinary techniques, the ultimate legitimation of the citizen. And yet work is also the very expression of subjugation, of the docilization of the subject. It is at the heart of the general diffusion of the "political anatomy" (*Discipline* 28) carried out by the ancien régime.

As Foucault observes, discipline was the only form of subjectification available during the Enlightenment. Such docilization requires submission to a series of techniques of normalization, an active response to coercive mechanisms and behavioral regulations, integration into a hierarchy of power, obedience to procedures of punishment and various forms of regimentation. Under such repressive onslaughts, the individual becomes the scientific-disciplinary atom of the mercantile society.

Foucault has been criticized for not studying forms of resistance to discipline and, instead, developing a totalizing model that does not allow for the possibility of challenge. In an analysis of Rousseau's *Rêveries*, I examine a subjectification that escapes the grip of the technology of power operating during the period. Moreover, I show how Rousseau, the dissident author par excellence of the Enlightenment, constructs an existence that evades the system of discipline and in so doing avoids the traps of usefulness and functionality. Indeed, the Rousseau of the *Rêveries* can be seen as the supreme fictional hero of the "genealogy of resistance" that Foucault has been taken to task for not writing (Best and Kellner 70). Foucault's perspective, which can be offered as an ideological interpretation of Rousseau's autobiographical text, allows, at the same time, for a revision of Foucault's own propositions on the Enlightenment.

Rousseau's *Rêveries*, written toward the end of his life, presents an interesting attempt at producing a different kind of body, one freed from all constraint and unfettered by any relation to knowledge or power. Indeed, Rousseau goes about meticulously undoing each link in the chain of the disciplined body. The *Rêveries* reproduces, but in an inverted form, the mechanism of control of the subject. Rousseau's autobiographical aim must be understood as an attempt to create an apolitical and "ventilated" individualization, one detached from all sites of power—indeed, from all relations. This is what Rousseau calls his "desœuvrement" (1000) ("desuetude" [7]), an effort to disengage the body, ventilate its materiality, and objectively nullify his person.

It is probably the Fifth Walk that offers the best illustration of Rousseau's new attitude and in which he best reveals the nature of the useless subject. What has most often been taken as a sketch of the autonomous individual can be understood as the depiction of the asceticism of an individual freed from temporal constraints. Rousseau abandons measured time; his walk is unscheduled, given over to caprice, to the idiosyncratic activity of the individual. He evokes a suspended time: "le présent dure toujours sans neanmoins marquer sa durée et sans aucune trace de succession" (1046) ("the present lasts forever without, however, making its duration noticed and without any trace of time's passage" [46]). Thus Rousseau recounts his joy on the Island of Saint-Pierre, his feeling of delightful retirement:

Le précieux *far niente* fut la premiére et la principale de ces jouissances que je voulus savourer dans toute sa douceur, et tout ce que je fis durant mon séjour ne fut en effet que l'occupation délicieuse et necessaire d'un homme qui s'est dévoué à l'oisiveté.   (1042)

The precious *far niente* was the first and the principal enjoyment I wanted to savor in all its sweetness, and all I did during my sojourn was in effect only the delightful and necessary pursuit of a man who has devoted himself to idleness.   (42)

Rest, which is the foundation of pleasure, is the opposite of work and production. The cultivation of the self depends here on pure sloth, on the ability to forget utilitarian action. *To do nothing* means to refuse the world's materiality in favor of an inner investment: "Le mouvement qui ne vient pas du dehors se fait alors au dedans de nous" (1048) ("Movement which does not come from outside then occurs inside us" [47]). Rousseau also seeks to release the soul from the body's imprisonment. The aim of the solitary's enterprise is not only the liberation of the subjugated organism but also an existential freedom. Laziness, as a means of effacing the outside world, allows for the development of the inner life, of pure psychic activity. And even psychic life is subjected to the minimum of constraints. Reasoning is abandoned. Immediate affection and emotion-based memory dominate. Ultimately, even the activity of writing is destined to idleness. In the absence of any requirement, the notation of a reverie or a walk is itself subject to the rule of *far niente*, of absolute amusement—that is, to viewing activity as a waste of time: in its very conception, the *Rêveries* is doomed to the incompletion with which it ends.

Later, in the Seventh Walk, Rousseau puts forth botany as the walker's exemplary activity: "La botanique est l'étude d'un oisif et paresseux solitaire" ("Botany is a study for an idle and lazy solitary person"). And he adds, "Il y a dans cette oiseuse occupation un charme qu'on ne sent que dans le plein calme des passions" (1069) ("In this idle occupation there is a charm we feel only in the complete calm of the passions" [64]). What is it about botany that captivates him? As Rousseau sees it, the botanist's activity is fundamentally disinterested; it demands the least possible corporeal effort. Botanical wandering is an act of pure looking, observation without profit or any instructional aim. Rousseau had started by eliminating other activities because of their ability to produce constraint, of forcing the organism's extensive attachment to a single activity. Indeed, he rejects all forms of knowledge with an industrial application. Botany's advantage is that it stands outside the utilitarian hierarchy of techniques. Thus mineralogy is criticized because of its nefarious requirements:

Pour profiter dans l'étude des mineraux, il faut être chymiste et physicien; il faut faire des expériences pénibles et couteuses, travailler dans

des laboratoires, dépenser beaucoup d'argent et de tems parmi le char-
bon, les creusets, les fourneaux, les cornues, dans la fumée et les vapeurs
étouffantes, toujours au risque de sa vie et souvent aux dépends de sa
santé.   (1067)

To make progress in the study of minerals, it is necessary to be a chemist
and a physicist. It is necessary to perform tedious and costly experi-
ments, to work in laboratories, to spend much money and time in the
midst of charcoal, crucibles, furnaces, retorts, smoke, and suffocating
fumes, always at the risk of life and often at the expense of health.
                                                                            (63)

The study of the animal kingdom is subject to similar objections:

Comment observer, dissequer, étudier, connoitre les oiseaux dans les
airs, les poissons dans les eaux, les quadrupedes plus legers que le vent,
plus forts que l'homme et qui ne sont pas plus disposés à venir s'offrir
à mes recherches que moi de courir après eux pour les y soumettre de
force?   (1067–68)

How am I to observe, dissect, study, become acquainted with the birds
in the air, the fish in the water, or the quadrupeds swifter than the wind
and stronger than man, which are no more disposed to come offer themselves to my research than I to run after them to make them submit to
it by force?   (63)

Unlike these two areas of investigation, botany imposes nothing on the body;
instrumentality plays no role here. The botanist's tools require no codification
of the body: "une pointe et une loupe sont tout l'appareil dont il a besoin"
(1069) ("a point and a magnifying glass are all the apparatus he needs" [64]).
Such equipment is a nonconstraining extension of the organs they supplement—in this case, the eye and the hand.

Indeed, one of the most unusual moments in the *Rêveries* occurs in the
Seventh Walk, when Rousseau, the solitary plant collector, finds himself at the
doors of a stocking factory. Obviously this episode can be read as
the subconscious reactivation of Rousseau's paranoia, his rediscovery of his
human persecutors in what should be a place of perfect seclusion and refuge.
And yet how ironic is this encounter between the lazy botanist and a mill full
of workers! Rousseau's reverie is interrupted by "un certain cliquetis" (1071)
("a certain clanking" [66]), the regular sound of the factory, labor's rhythmic
cadence: in fact, it is the machine itself. The anonymous industrial apparatus,
the uncanny murmur of "l'industrie humaine" (1072) ("human industry" [66])
startles Rousseau:

Surpris et curieux je me léve, je perce à travers un fourré de broussaille du coté d'où venoit le bruit, et dans une combe à vingt pas du lieu même où je croyois être parvenu le prémier j'apperçois une manufacture de bas.   (1071)

Surprised and curious, I got up, burst through a thicket of brush on the side from which the noise was coming, and, in a little hollow twenty feet from the very place where I had believed myself to have been the first to arrive, I saw a stocking mill.   (66)

The *Rêveries* presents us with a portrait of the ascetic self in its evasion of constraint. What we must see in Rousseau's project of retirement, as he conceived it near the end of his life, is the wearying demand for liberty. If this is a text written against the Enlightenment and its philosophers, then the roots of this critique are in the heroization of a languorous liberty: "je ne pouvois souffrir l'assujetissement, j'étois parfaitement libre, et mieux que libre, car assujeti par mes seuls attachemens, je ne faisois que ce que je voulois faire" (1099) ("I could not bear subjection; I was perfectly free and better than free, for bound only by my affections, I did only what I wanted to do" [90]). The subject renounces the sphere of activity; he revels in not-doing: "Je m'abstiens d'agir: car toute ma foiblesse est pour l'action, toute ma force est négative" (1059) ("I abstain from acting, for all my weakness is with regard to action, all my strength is negative" [56]). As such, Rousseau sets himself in opposition to his contemporaries, who are compulsive "actifs, remuans" ("busy, restless" people). The "scandal" of Jean-Jacques's liberty is to be understood in the movement of a double restriction imposed by the subject "ne jamais faire ce qu'il ne veut pas" (1059) ("never doing what he does not want to do" [56]).

Rousseau's arrested *vita otiosa* leaves behind the world of automatons otherwise promoted by the eighteenth century. The *Rêveries* can be read as a strange version of La Mettrie's *L'Homme-machine* (*Man a Machine*), presenting this time, however, the body's inability to conform to hierarchy and power or to utilitarian synthesis. Rousseau's project of laziness rejects industriousness as uncontested positivity or the sole destiny of man and civilization.

Translated by Thomas Epstein

Reading Rousseau's Women:
Autobiography and Femininity
in the *Confessions*

Christine Roulston

In Rousseau's *Confessions*, women are not only in plentiful supply as characters but they also offer a way of interpreting Rousseau's relation to the process of autobiography. The representation of femininity, therefore, informs his larger project of self-revelation and transparency. The narrator is willing to examine and to reveal his desire: from his sexual proclivities (the episode of the spanking) to his passionate and idealized love for Mme d'Houdetot. By providing the ground for self-revelation, these encounters with the feminine confirm Rousseau's search for "un homme dans toute la vérité de la nature" (5) ("a man in all the truth of nature" [5]).

And yet we know from Rousseau's other writings that femininity is not the source of truth but rather of deception, disguise, and dissimulation. What Linda M. G. Zerilli refers to as "the masquerade of femininity" (21) determines Rousseau's approach to the analysis of gender. Repeatedly, women are presented as a threat to orderliness, to republican ideals, and ultimately to manhood. What Rousseau seems to fear, above all, is the collapse of gender difference and the eventual revelation that, in Zerilli's words, "natural man and woman are pedagogical constructions and highly unstable ones at that" (18). For Rousseau, the erasing of gender difference inevitably leads to feminization, to a dissolving of boundaries and the return to the mother and the womb.

This return to the mother raises again the question of autobiography. As a narrative form, it aims to go back to the beginning, with the narrator's birth, one that can be neither remembered nor known. Thus autobiography is founded on a fictional origin, a story rather than a history. In Rousseau's case, the fact that his mother died nine days after giving birth to him increases this sense of fictionality: "Dix mois après, je naquis infirme et malade; je coûtai la vie à ma mere, et ma naissance fut le premier de mes malheurs" (7) ("Ten months later, I was born feeble and sickly; I cost my mother her life, and my birth was the first of my misfortunes" [6]). By definition, Rousseau's mother can be located only in the realms of the imagination and the fictional—a site that explains, to some degree, the writer's ongoing anxiety with regard to women. We can interpret the founding narrative of loss as structuring the different ways in which women figure in the text of the *Confessions*. In an intriguing act of substitution, the mother dies as if to give place to fiction:

je ne me souviens que de mes prémiéres lectures et de leur effet sur moi: c'est le tems d'où je date sans interruption la conscience de moi-

même. Ma mère avoit laissé des Romans. Nous nous mimes à les lire
après soupé mon pere et moi.   (8)

I remember only my first readings and their effect on me. This is the
time from which I date the uninterrupted consciousness of myself. My
mother had left behind some Novels. My father and I began to read
them after supper.   (7)

Here, autobiographical memory is both recovered and covered over by the
act of reading the mother's novels. The mother becomes the indirect purveyor
of an irresponsible pedagogy—"cette dangereuse methode" (8) ("this dangerous method" [7])—one by which Rousseau the young boy is entirely seduced.
    Rousseau's autobiographical narrative replays, in significant ways, the initial
association between women and novels, or femininity and the imagination.
When Mme d'Houdetot makes her first visit to Rousseau at the Ermitage on
Mme d'Epinay's property, the novel is directly invoked as a means of articu-
lating the experience of seduction: "Au plus fort de mes douces rêveries j'eus
une visite de Mad^e d'Houdetot. . . . Cette visite eut un peu l'air d'un début de
roman" (431–32) ("At the height of my sweet reveries, I had a visit from Mme
d'Houdetot. . . . This visit had a little of the air of the beginning of a novel"
[363]). Sophie enters Rousseau's reveries rather than his material world. This
encounter is radically mediated by the fictionalizing process. As the romance
advances, so does the fusion between Rousseau's fictional character Julie—
the heroine of the novel he is composing at the time—and Mme d'Houdetot:
"j'étois ivre d'amour sans objet, cette ivresse fascina mes yeux, cet objet se
fixa sur elle, je vis ma Julie en Mad^e d'Houdetot" (440) ("I was intoxicated
with love without an object. That intoxication fascinated my eyes, that object
became fixed on her, I saw my Julie in Mme d'Houdetot" [370]). As fiction
supplements experience, Mme d'Houdetot acquires signification through the
figure of Julie, so much so that it is unclear whether Rousseau would have
desired Mme d'Houdetot if Julie did not exist.
    Peggy Kamuf de Magnin claims that Rousseau's desire in the *Confessions*
is predicated on the idea that less is more (166). For Rousseau, fulfillment is,
paradoxically, experienced through its lack. Rousseau's emotions are at their
most intense when he is either physically or symbolically separated from the
object of his desire. He writes the following about Mme Basile, one of his
early loves: "Rien de tout ce que m'a fait sentir la possession des femmes ne
vaut les deux minutes que j'ai passées à ses pieds sans même oser toucher à
sa robe" (76–77) ("Nothing of all the feelings caused in me by the possession
of women is worth the two minutes I spent at her feet without even daring
to touch her dress" [64]). Sophie d'Houdetot is described in parallel fashion:
"La véhémence de ma passion la contenoit par elle-même. . . . Je l'aimois
trop pour vouloir la posséder" (444) ("The vehemence of my passion kept it

contained all by itself. . . . I loved her too much to want to possess her" [373]). Nonpossession becomes more complete than possession: less is more.

Desire, for Rousseau, must be a mediated experience, one in which the object—namely, the female body—is never fully revealed. Just as Rousseau's founding memory is located in the act of reading that, as he tells us himself, is never effectively replaced by experience, so his desire is expressed by means of the fetish or the synecdoche. Rousseau writes of his sexual preferences:

> D'ailleurs des couturiéres, des filles de chambre, de petites marchandes ne me tentoient guéres. Il me falloit des Demoiselles. Chacun a ses fantaisies; ç'a toujours été la mienne. . . . Ce n'est pourtant pas du tout la vanité de l'état et du rang qui m'attire; c'est un teint mieux conservé, de plus belles mains . . . une robe plus fine et mieux faite, une chaussure plus mignone, des rubans. . . . Je trouve moi-même cette préférence très ridicule; mais mon cœur la donne malgré moi.   (134)

> Moreover, dressmakers, chambermaids, little tradeswomen hardly tempted me. I needed young Ladies. Each has his whims; that has always been mine. . . . However, it is not at all vanity of status and rank that attracts me; it is a better preserved complexion, more beautiful hands . . . a more delicate and better-made dress, a daintier shoe, ribbons. . . . I myself find this preference very ridiculous; but my heart bestows it in spite of me.   (112–13)

This list unfolds in a revealing manner: from women defined by their profession, working and hence working-class subjects, to whom Rousseau is not attracted, to "young Ladies" defined by their appearance and their attire, and hence fragmented and fetishized. They are women of leisure, with the time to preen and to be admired. While there is little evidence that Rousseau was attracted by money, he is nevertheless drawn to a type of femininity that only the middle and upper classes can afford. The well-dressed "young Ladies," furthermore, do not reveal too much. Rousseau's emphasis on clothes and ornamentation, on surfaces, reveals, in turn, his obsession with modesty— hence the focus on a hand, a shoe, a ribbon. The well-groomed "young Ladies" can remain mysterious, and thereby allow Rousseau's imagination free rein. Indeed, Rousseau's desire for modesty in women, which he often talks about, is perhaps tied less to the question of virtue than to that of desire. While Rousseau observes appearances and critiques the fact that society is never as it seems, he needs, above all, the appearance of modesty—and the tantalizing possibility of what it can reveal—to structure his desire.

The only time Rousseau describes the sexual act with a woman he loves, Mme de Warens, he presents it as a spectacular failure, a source of dread and disgust: "Comment, par quel prodige dans la fleur de ma jeunesse eus-je si peu d'empressement pour la prémiere jouissance? . . . Comment au lieu des délices qui devoient m'enivrer sentois-je presque de la répugnance et des craintes?" (195) ("How, by what prodigy could I have so little eagerness for the first enjoyment in the flower of my youth? . . . How instead of delights that should have intoxicated me did I feel almost repugnance and fears?" [164]). In this case, the equation has been reversed; more (his happiness) has become less (repugnance and fears). The question arises: What has Rousseau lost by this gain of sexual experience? He answers this himself: "elle étoit pour moi plus qu'une sœur, plus qu'une mere, plus qu'une amie, plus même qu'une maîtresse. . . . Enfin je l'aimois trop pour la convoiter: voila ce qu'il y a de plus clair dans mes idées" (196–97) ("For me she was more than a sister, more than a mother, more than a friend, even more than a mistress, and it was for that reason that she was not a mistress. In sum, I loved her too much to covet her: that is what is clearest in my ideas" [165]). The multiple relationships Rousseau has enjoyed with Mme de Warens would be reduced to the one if she were his mistress. As with Mme Basile and Sophie d'Houdetot, Rousseau wants to hold on to the factor of "more than," of excess through nonpossession. What women can be imagined to be is far more intriguing than what they are. In contrast to the figure of the libertine, who wants to prove the exchangeability of women through repeated seductions, Rousseau avoids seduction to keep his fictions in place.

While Rousseau controls women by means of his imagination, he also wants to be mastered by them, to be in a position of surrender. As Joel Schwartz has argued, "women pose the greatest threat to Rousseau's quest for solitude. For like Emile he is inclined to depend upon women, and to enjoy depending upon them" (99). Many of Rousseau's theoretical writings on the dangers of feminization point to an anxiety that can be mapped out in the *Confessions*. Rousseau situates himself in a passive, and hence conventionally feminine, position with regard to most of the women he desires. He relishes being spanked (Mlle Lambercier); being taken prisoner (the adventure with Mlle de Graffenried and Mlle Galley); being a son, a pupil, a servant—he describes himself, among other things, as "l'ouvrage, l'elève" (58) ("the product, student" [48]) of Mme de Warens, whom he also calls "Mamma." Women are potentially so dangerous for Rousseau because he becomes feminized in their presence, a situation that threatens to collapse the gender distinctions he is so eager to uphold as a theorist. Rousseau's relationships with women expose his conflicted relation to masculinity; in a sense, the *Confessions* describes the ways in which Rousseau is not a man. While his other works attempt to establish codes of manhood, of ideal citizenry and patriarchal pride, the *Confessions* attests to Rousseau's many failures as a masculinized subject. Rousseau at once loves women and loves being in the position of the woman.

Such a reading gives us some indication as to why Rousseau chooses Thérèse Levasseur as his lifelong companion, for her remarkable invisibility in the *Confessions* suggests her failure to constitute any kind of female threat for its author. In many ways, Thérèse embodies the concept of lack; though Rousseau was to marry her in 1768, in the *Confessions* she never achieves the status of wife: "Je lui déclarai davance que je ne l'abandonnerois ni ne l'épouserois jamais" (331) ("I declared to her in advance that I would never either abandon her or marry her" [278]), and she fails to leave a mark or a trace in Rousseau's text. The only way she does signify is through mis-signification: "Autrefois j'avois fait un dictionnaire de ses phrases pour amuser Mad⁣ᵉ de Luxembourg, et ses qui-pro-quo sont devenus célébres dans les so-cietés où j'ai vécu" (332) ("In the past I had a dictionary of her sayings made up to amuse Mme de Luxembourg, and her malapropisms have become fa-mous in the social circles in which I have lived" [279]). Thérèse's access to representation is through her misuse of language, another variant on poor female pedagogy. While Rousseau's mother left him "dangerous" novels, Thé-rèse leaves behind linguistic blunders, each one a distortion of the proper use of the sign. Thérèse enters the *Confessions* as a secondary figure, a replace-ment for Mamma; she functions as an adjunct, an extension that allows Rous-seau to operate as if, in fact, he were alone. While he writes that "je trouvois dans Therese le supplement dont j'avois besoin" (332) ("in Thérèse I found the supplement I needed" [278]), it is actually Thérèse who is supplemented. Presented as neither a wife nor a mother—her five children are given up for adoption by Rousseau—Thérèse is the "less than" who has to be added to, an absent presence who allows Rousseau to put other things in her place: his work or other women. With Thérèse, Rousseau can function unhindered as an artist, a fictional lover, and a lover of fictions.

APPENDIX

A Brief Chronology of Rousseau's Life, with Selected Corresponding Page References from the *Confessions* and *Rêveries*

Emphasis in the following list is given to the scenes and events referred to in this volume. The chronology draws in large part on that published in *Œuvres complètes* 1: ci–cxviii and on Raymond Trousson and Frédéric S. Eigeldinger's *Jean-Jacques Rousseau au jour le jour: chronologie*. The reader wishing fuller accounts may consult these sources. *Conf.* and *Rêv.* are in *OC* 1.

1712   Jean-Jacques Rousseau, son of Isaac Rousseau and Suzanne Bernard, is born on 28 June in Geneva, at 40 Grand'rue. Rousseau's mother dies nine days later, on 7 July.

1722   Rousseau's father leaves Geneva for Nyon. In October the young Jean-Jacques moves into the home of the Lambercier family, relatives who live in Bossey, outside Geneva (*Conf.* 12–24 [*CW* 5: 11–21]). The spanking, broken comb, and walnut tree episodes occur in late October (*Conf.* 14–16; 18–21; 22–24 [*CW* 5: 12–14; 16–18; 19–21]). (See the essay by McDonald.)

1724–25   Jean-Jacques moves back to Geneva, to stay with his uncle for the winter.

1728   Rousseau, who has worked as an apprentice for the engraver Ducommun since spring 1725, returns to the city one day after a walk. He finds its gates closed and decides to leave his native city on 15 March (*Conf.* 30–42 [*CW* 5: 25–35]). A week later, he arrives in Annecy, in the French Alps, at the home of Mme de Warens, to whom he has been recommended by a pastor. He meets her on Palm Sunday, 21 March (*Conf.* 48–54 [*CW* 5: 40–45]). After only a few days, Rousseau leaves for Turin, in the Italian Piedmont. There he converts to Catholicism and serves as a footman for Mme de Vercellis. The stolen ribbon episode takes place here, on 25 December (*Conf.* 84–87 [*CW* 5: 70–73]).

1729–31   Rousseau comes and goes at Mme de Warens's house at Annecy. Officially, he does secretarial work and prepares medicines for Mme de Warens, but the two soon begin an amorous relationship. Rousseau moves into her house at Chambéry in September 1731. The cherry-picking scene with Mlle de Graffenried and Mlle Galley occurs in early July 1730 (*OC* 1: 135–39 [*CW* 5: 113–16]). His music apprenticeship with M. Le Maître extends from late October 1729 to mid-April 1730 (*Conf.* 121–30 [*CW* 5: 102–09]).

1736   Rousseau has his first idyllic stay at Les Charmettes, the country house at the Chambéry city limits that Mme de Warens begins renting at the end of the summer (*Conf.* 224–36 [*CW* 5: 187–98]).

1738   Rousseau returns to Chambéry after a trip to Montpellier. He receives a cold greeting from Mme de Warens, who has taken another lover. (See the essay by Herbold.)

1740   Rousseau is in Lyon as a tutor for M. de Mably's two sons (*Conf.* 267–70 [*CW* 5: 223–26]). He returns to Chambéry in 1741.

1742   Rousseau reads his *Projet concernant de nouveaux signes pour la musique* at the Académie des Sciences in Paris and is commended for his work. The event marks his entry into the intellectual world.

1743   Rousseau leaves Paris for Venice. He serves there as secretary to the French ambassador, the count de Montaigu, for a year, then returns to Paris. The quarrel with Montaigu takes place between 20 January and 10 February 1744 (*Conf.* 308–13 [*CW* 5: 258–63]).

1745   Rousseau comes to know Thérèse Levasseur, a linen maid from Orléans, with whom he will spend a great deal of his life and have five children, all of whom were turned over to orphanages. He would marry her in 1768. Rousseau meets Diderot and Condillac and exchanges letters with Voltaire. (See the essay by Roulston.)

1749   Rousseau writes several articles on music for the *Encyclopédie*.

1750   The Académie de Dijon awards its prize for best essay to Rousseau for his first *Discours*, which is published at the end of the year.

1752   Rousseau stays for a few days with Mme d'Epinay at La Chevrette, her home at Montmorency in the Val-d'Oise region outside Paris.

1754   Rousseau reestablishes his Genevan citizenship and returns to the Protestant faith.

1755   The second *Discours* is published. Rousseau goes back to La Chevrette for another stay and decides to move there the following year, living in a small lodging on the property known as the Ermitage (or Hermitage).

1757   Mme d'Houdetot begins visiting Rousseau at the Ermitage in early

January (*Conf.* 432–33; 438–48 [*CW* 5: 363–64; 369–76]). Rousseau falls in love, platonically, with the countess, who partly inspires the creation of his fictional character Julie. After a falling out with Mme d'Epinay, Rousseau moves to Montlouis, a small residence with a garden in Montmorency. (See the essay by Roulston.)

1761   *Julie, ou la Nouvelle Héloïse* is published.

1762   Two of Rousseau's works are published: *Du contrat social*, then *Emile*, which is condemned. A warrant is issued for Rousseau's arrest. He flees France for Yverdon, near Bern, where a similar fate awaits him. He renounces his Genevan citizenship and, in late August, begins wearing Armenian attire (*Conf.* 600–01 [*CW* 5: 502–03]).

1764   Rousseau decides to write his *Confessions*.

1765   His house at Môtiers, to which he moves after leaving Yverdon, is stoned on 6 September (*Conf.* 634–36 [*CW* 5: 531–33]). He spends ten days in July on the Island of Saint-Pierre, in Lake Bienne (Neuchâtel region). He returns in September to the island, the setting for several reveries (*Conf.* 614 [*CW* 5: 514]; *Rêv.* 1040–49 [*CW* 8: 41–48]). He leaves the island on 25 or 26 October. Rousseau returns triumphantly to Paris at the end of the year. (See the essays by O'Neal and Saint-Amand.)

1766   Rousseau begins writing the *Confessions* while he is in England.

1770   He finishes the *Confessions* in December and begins holding private readings of his manuscript (*Conf.* 656 [*CW* 5: 550]).

1772   Rousseau starts writing the *Dialogues*.

1776   On 24 February, Rousseau attempts to leave a copy of the *Dialogues* on the altar of Notre-Dame cathedral but finds the gates locked (*Dialogues* 979–80 [*CW* 1: 248]). In the early fall, he writes the first and second chapters, or Walks, of *Les Rêveries du promeneur solitaire*. On 24 October, while returning to Paris from a walk, he is run over by a Great Dane in Ménilmontant (*Rêv.* 1003–066 [*CW* 8: 10–13]). The Ninth Walk is not completed until March 1778. The Tenth Walk is left unfinished.

1778   The marquis de Girardin invites Rousseau to stay with him at Ermenonville, north of Paris. Rousseau accepts the offer and moves there with Thérèse. He dies at Ermenonville on 2 July and is buried on the Ile des peupliers (Island of Poplar Trees) on the property.

1782   Moultou and Du Peyrou publish the *Collection complète des œuvres de J. J. Rousseau, citoyen de Genève*, containing the *Confessions* and the *Rêveries*. (See the essay by Trousson.)

1794   The remains of Rousseau, who has become a hero to the French revolutionaries, are transferred to the Pantheon in Paris.

An Annotated List of Rousseau's Other Works Mentioned in the Essays (and Discussed in the *Confessions*)

1750   First *Discours*, or *Discours sur les sciences et les arts* (*OC* 1: 350–52; 365–67 [*CW* 5: 294–96; 306–08]): The essay that won the Académie de Dijon's prize and established Rousseau as an important, albeit controversial, intellectual. In this essay, Rousseau introduces his thesis that, far from perfecting humans, the arts and sciences—that is, culture and society in general—have corrupted them.

1752   *Le Devin du village* (*The Village Soothsayer*) (*OC* 1: 374–83 [*CW* 5: 314–22]): Rousseau's opera, highly successful early in his career and performed at Fontainebleau for King Louis XV, who offers Rousseau a pension. By his refusal to appear before the king, however Rousseau gives up the pension.

1755   Second *Discours*, or *Discours sur l'origine et les fondements de l'inégalité parmi les hommes* (*OC* 1: 388–89; 392–95 [*CW* 5: 326; 329–32]): The work that pursues the same line of thinking as the first *Discours* but elaborates on the process by which human beings have fallen from an original state of goodness in nature. Inequality is traced to the first person's claim to property.

1758   *Lettre à d'Alembert sur les spectacles* (*OC* 1: 494–98; 501–02 [*CW* 5: 414–17; 420–21]): A response to d'Alembert's *Encyclopédie* article "Genève," in which the writer proposes a national theater for the city of Rousseau's birth. Rousseau, who strongly opposes any such formal institution, considers public fetes to be more virtuous and useful gatherings of citizens than plays (*spectacles*) are.

1761   *Julie, ou la Nouvelle Héloïse* (*OC* 1: 430–38; 544–48 [*CW* 5: 361–67; 456–58]): An eighteenth-century best-seller that propounds the fundamental sensibility, and therefore equality, of all human beings. The novel depicts a small, virtuous society or moral elite in an idyllic country setting in Switzerland.

1762   *Du contrat social* (*OC* 1: 571; 590–92 [*CW* 5: 478; 494–95]): A portrayal of human freedom as a birthright that degenerates into dependence, if not slavery, in society. The work outlines Rousseau's notion of the general will and the democratic principle of the people's sovereignty.

1762   *Emile, ou De l'éducation* (*OC* 1: 534–35; 573–75 [*CW* 5: 447–48; 479–82]): Part pedagogical treatise, part novel. In this work, which presents Rousseau's negative educational theory, the eponymous young protagonist is kept away from the supposedly pernicious forces of society for as long as possible through the careful guidance of his tutor. *Emile* advocates a domestic role for women, who are encouraged to breast-feed their children rather than to employ wet nurses. The *Profession de foi du vicaire savoyard* is included in book 4 of *Emile*.

1762   *Lettre à Christophe de Beaumont* (*OC* 1: 606 [*CW* 5: 507]): A communication to the archbishop of Paris after the condemnation of both *Emile*, publicly burned on 11 June, and the *Contrat social*, which received similar treatment from Geneva's governing council on 19 June. Rousseau responds to the accusation of heresy leveled at *Emile* for several reasons, but notably for its defense of natural religion over traditional, "revealed" religion.

1764   *Lettres écrites de la montagne* (*OC* 1: 610; 623–28 [*CW* 5: 510–11; 522–26]): Another response to the condemnation of *Emile* and the *Contrat social* by Geneva's governing council in 1762. In addition to defending his person and his work, Rousseau analyzes the political and religious controversies in Geneva. The work was burned in The Hague and in Paris.

Like the *Confessions* and the *Rêveries*, the following works were published posthumously:

1779   *Lettres à Malesherbes*: Four autobiographical letters written in 1762 to the state censor in France (whose official title was "directeur de la Librairie") to defend the integrity of his character.

1782   *Lettres sur la botanique*: Eight letters written for Mme Delessert between 1771 and 1773 and before the *Rêveries*. This work has a more scientific and pedagogical angle than its literary counterpart.

1782   *Rousseau juge de Jean Jaques, Dialogues*: Rousseau's further attempt to exculpate himself through an elaborate literary doubling of his character. Composed after the *Confessions* and before the *Rêveries*, the work presents the writer as an innocent victim, greatly misunderstood by the public, which itself is being misled by a league of conspirators. The first *Dialogue* is published in England in 1780; the manuscript in its entirety is included in the *Collection complète des œuvres de J. J. Rousseau*, published by Moultou and Du Peyrou (1782).

1908   *Mon Portrait*: A series of autobiographical fragments, written between 1756 and 1762 and published in part during the nineteenth century and as a whole in the early twentieth century.

NOTES ON CONTRIBUTORS

Mary Ellen Birkett is professor of French language and literature at Smith College. She is the author of *Lamartine and the Poetics of Landscape* (1982) and has conducted research on French diplomacy in the Pacific, particularly in the Hawaiian Islands, in the first half of the nineteenth century. Her articles have appeared in the *Hawaiian Journal of History*, *Romance Notes*, *Kentucky Romance Quarterly*, *Modern Language Studies*, *Symposium*, *Stanford French Review*, *French Review*, *Romantisme*, and elsewhere. She contributed the essay "A Romantic Approach to Teaching Stendhal's *The Red and the Black*" to *Approaches to Teaching Stendhal's* The Red and the Black (1999).

Lorraine J. Clark is associate professor of English at Trent University (Canada). Author of *Blake, Kierkegaard, and the Spectre of Dialectic* (1991), she has coedited, with Guy LaFrance, *Rousseau and Criticism / Rousseau et la critique* (1995). Her article "Rousseau and Political Compassion in *The Nigger of the* Narcissus appeared in 1999 in *Conradiana*.

Patrick Coleman is professor of French and francophone studies at the University of California, Los Angeles. His publications include *Reparative Realism: Mourning and Modernity in the French Novel, 1730–1830* (1998); *The Limits of Sympathy: Gabrielle Roy's* The Tin Flute (1993); and *Rousseau's Political Imagination: Rule and Representation in the* Lettre à d'Alembert (1984). He has brought out editions of Rousseau's *Confessions* (2000) and *Discourse on Inequality* (1994) and Benjamin Constant's *Adolphe* (2001). With Jayne Lewis and Jill Kowalik, Coleman coedited a collection of essays, *Representations of the Self from the Renaissance to Romanticism* (2000) and, with David W. Carrithers, coedited *Montesquieu and Modernity* (2002).

Carl Fisher is professor of comparative literature at California State University, Long Beach. His publications include articles on Daniel Defoe and public disorder, William Godwin and the public sphere, Laurence Sterne and eighteenth-century educational theory, and representations of the pig in eighteenth-century literature. He and Maximillian Novak are the coeditors of another MLA volume, *Approaches to Teaching Robinson Crusoe* (in progress). Fisher is also coeditor, with Clorinda Donato, of the book review section of *Eighteenth-Century Studies*.

Sarah Herbold is lecturer in the Department of Comparative Literature at the University of California, Berkeley. She has published two other articles on Rousseau: "The *Confessions* and the Imagined Woman Reader" in *Eighteenth-Century Studies* (1999) and "Well-Placed Reflections: (Post)Modern Woman as a Symptom of (Post)Modern Man" in *Signs: A Journal of Women in Culture and Society* (1995). Her research and teaching interests center on the history and theory of the novel and on feminist theory.

Marie-Hélène Huet is Taylor Pyne Professor of French at Princeton University. Her publications include *Mourning Glory: The Will of the French Revolution* (1997), *Monstrous Imagination* (1993), *Rehearsing the Revolution: The Staging of Marat's Death, 1793–1797* (1982), *Le Héros et son double* (1975), and *L'Histoire des voyages extraordinaires* (1973).

Guillemette Johnston is professor of modern languages at DePaul University. Author of *Lectures poétiques: la représentation poétique du discours théorique chez Jean-Jacques Rousseau* (1996), she is also coeditor, with Tanguy L'Aminot, of the special issue *Rousseau et spiritualité* of *Etudes Jean-Jacques Rousseau* (1998). Her articles on Rousseau have appeared in the journals *Studies on Voltaire and the Eighteenth Century*, *Etudes Jean-Jacques Rousseau*, *Pensée Libre*, *Utah Foreign Languages Review*, and *Studies in Modern and Classical Languages and Literatures*, and in a collection of essays, *Jean-Jacques Rousseau, politique et nation*.

Thomas M. Kavanagh is professor of French at Yale University. He has written *Esthetics of the Moment: Literature and Art in the French Enlightenment* (1996), *Enlightenment and the Shadows of Chance* (1993), and *Writing in Truth: Authority and Desire in Rousseau* (1987).

Christopher Kelly is professor of political science at Boston College. With Roger D. Masters, he serves as series editor of *The Collected Writings of Rousseau*, published by the University Press of New England. He is the author of *Rousseau's Exemplary Life: The Confessions as Political Philosophy* (1987) and *Rousseau as Author: Consecrating One's Life to the Truth* (2003).

Christie McDonald is Smith Professor of the French Language and Literature and chair of the Department of Romance Languages and Literatures at Harvard University. She is the author of two studies as well as many articles on Rousseau, including *The Extravagant Shepherd: A Study of the Pastoral Vision in Rousseau's* Nouvelle Héloïse (1973) and *The Dialogue of Writing: Essays in Eighteenth-Century Literature* (1985). She has also written *Dispositions: textes et musique* (1986), *The Proustian Fabric* (1991), and co-edited *Transpositions* (1993).

Ourida Mostefai is associate professor of French at Boston College. She is the editor of *Lectures de* La Nouvelle Héloïse / *Reading* La Nouvelle Héloïse *Today* (1993) and the author of *Le Citoyen de Genève et la République des Lettres: etude de la controverse autour de la* Lettre à d'Alembert *de Jean-Jacques Rousseau* (2003). Mostefai has served as associate editor and editor of *Studies in Eighteenth-Century Culture*, as well as director of publications and past president of the Rousseau Association. She is a former president of the Society for Eighteenth-Century French Studies.

Michael O'Dea is professor in the Département des Lettres Modernes at the Université Lumière Lyon II. In addition to the book *Jean-Jacques Rousseau: Music, Illusion, and Desire* (1995), he has written articles on Rousseau, Diderot, eighteenth-century musical controversies, and aesthetic theory.

John C. O'Neal is professor of French at Hamilton College. His publications include *Changing Minds: The Shifting Perception of Culture in Eighteenth-Century France* (2002), *The Authority of Experience: Sensationist Theory in the French Enlightenment* (1996), and *Seeing and Observing: Rousseau's Rhetoric of Perception* (1985). O'Neal was named a Chevalier dans l'Ordre des Palmes Académiques in 1998 by the French minister of national education.

Jean Perkins is Susan W. Lippincott Professor Emerita of French at Swarthmore College. She has authored numerous articles in *Studies on Voltaire and the Eighteenth Century*, *Studies in Eighteenth-Century Culture*, *Diderot Studies*, *Annales Jean-Jacques*

Rousseau, and *Condorcet Studies*. She is past president of the Modern Language Association and the American Society for Eighteenth-Century Studies.

Christine Roulston is associate professor of French and women's studies at the University of Western Ontario. Her book *Virtue, Gender, and the Authentic Self in Eighteenth-Century Fiction: Richardson, Rousseau, and Laclos* appeared in 1998. She has published articles on Charlotte Lennox, Mme de Lafayette, Jane Austen, Mme de Graffigny, female friendship in the eighteenth century, and women and letters in the eighteenth century.

Pierre Saint-Amand is professor of French and comparative literature at Brown University. His publications include *The Laws of Hostility: Politics, Violence, and the Enlightenment* (1996), *The Libertine's Progress: Seduction in the Eighteenth-Century French Novel* (1994), and *Diderot: le labyrinthe de la relation* (1984). He has also edited three issues of *Stanford French Review*, on Diderot, the eighteenth-century novel, and autonomy in the Enlightenment.

Jean Starobinski is professor emeritus at the Université de Genève. Although best known for his highly influential *Jean-Jacques Rousseau: la transparence et l'obstacle* (1957), he has also written *L'Invention de la liberté* (1964), *La Relation critique* (1970; expanded ed. in 2001), *1789: les emblèmes de la raison* (1973), *Le Remède dans le mal* (1989), among many other books. His most recent work is *Action et Réaction: vie et aventures d'un couple* (1999). Starobinski is past president of the Société Jean-Jacques Rousseau (Geneva) and a member of the American Academy of Arts and Sciences and the British Academy.

Virginia E. Swain is associate professor of French at Dartmouth College. She is the author of *Grotesque Figures: Baudelaire, Rousseau, and the Esthetics of Modernity* (forthcoming from Johns Hopkins UP) and articles on Rousseau, Diderot, Baudelaire, and French women authors of the eighteenth century.

Raymond Trousson is professor emeritus at the Université Libre de Bruxelles. He is the author of numerous studies of Rousseau, including *Rousseau et sa fortune littéraire* (1977) and *Jean-Jacques Rousseau: heurs et malheurs d'une conscience* (1993). His most recent work on Rousseau is *Jean-Jacques Rousseau jugé par ses contemporains: du Discours sur le sciences et les arts aux Confessions* (2000). He is a member of the Académie Royale de Langue et de Littérature Françaises.

Byron R. Wells is professor of Romance languages at Wake Forest University. He has published a monograph on *Clarissa* and *La Nouvelle Héloïse* and coedited volumes of essays on the seventeenth and eighteenth centuries. A number of his articles have focused on Rousseau, and his current research interest is in Rousseau's political language. Wells has served as executive director of the American Society for Eighteenth-Century Studies since 1997.

SURVEY PARTICIPANTS

Nadine S. Bérenguier, *University of New Hampshire*
Mary Ellen Birkett, *Smith College*
Theodore E. D. Braun, *University of Delaware*
Yves Citton, *University of Pittsburgh*
Lorraine J. Clark, *Trent University, Canada*
Patrick Coleman, *University of California, Los Angeles*
Margery Crumpacker, *New York City*
Stephen Duguid, *Simon Fraser University, Canada*
Carl Fisher, *California State University, Long Beach*
Peter France, *University of Edinburgh, United Kingdom*
Anne F. Garréta, *Université de Haute Bretagne, France*
Pamela D. Gay-White, *Alabama State University, Montgomery*
Patrick Henry, *Whitman College*
Marie-Hélène Huet, *Princeton University*
Guillemette Johnston, *DePaul University*
Christopher Kelly, *Boston College*
Kurt Kloocke, *Universität Tübingen, Germany*
Ellen Marie Krefting, *University of Oslo, Norway*
Eugénia Pinto Leal, *Universidade Nova de Lisboa, Portugal*
Ricardo Monteagudo, *Universidade de São Paulo, Brazil*
Michael O'Dea, *Université Lumière Lyon II, France*
George W. Poe, *University of the South*
Adam Potkay, *College of William and Mary*
Christine Roulston, *University of Western Ontario, Canada*
Elena Russo, *Johns Hopkins University*
Junji Sato, *University of Hokkaido, Japan*
Norbert Sclippa, *College of Charleston*
Julia Simon, *Pennsylvania State University*
Virginia E. Swain, *Dartmouth College*
Downing A. Thomas, *University of Iowa*
Mary Trouille, *Illinois State University, Normal*

WORKS CITED

Alembert, Jean Le Rond d'. "Eloge de Milord Maréchal." Œuvres de d'Alembert. Vol. 3. Paris: Belin, 1821. 685–721.

Augustine, Saint. Confessions. Ed. and trans. Henry Chadwick. Oxford: Oxford UP, 1991.

Barruel-Beauvert, Antoine de. Vie de J.-J. Rousseau. London, 1789.

Baudelaire, Charles. Œuvres complètes. Ed. Claude Pichois. 2 vols. Paris: Gallimard, 1975–76.

Best, Steven, and Douglas Kellner. Postmodern Theory. New York: Guilford, 1991.

Blake, William. "London." The Complete Poetry and Prose of William Blake. Ed. David V. Erdman. Berkeley: U of California P, 1982. 26–27.

Bloom, Allan, ed. and trans. Emile; or, On Education. By Jean-Jacques Rousseau. New York: Basic, 1979.

Bonnet, Jean-Claude. "Le Fantasme de l'écrivain." Poétique 63 (1985): 259–77.

Bovier, Gaspard. Journal du séjour à Grenoble de Jean-Jacques Rousseau. Ed. Raymond Schiltz. Grenoble: Boissard, 1964.

Brooks, Peter. Troubling Confessions: Speaking Guilt in Law and Literature. Chicago: U of Chicago P, 2000.

Brooks, Richard A., ed. Supplement to Cabeen's Critical Bibliography. Syracuse: Syracuse UP, 1968.

Brunel, Pierre, et al. Histoire de la littérature française. Paris: Bordas, 1972.

Butterworth, Charles E., ed. The Reveries of the Solitary Walker. By Jean-Jacques Rousseau. Indianapolis: Hackett, 1992.

Cabeen, David Clark, ed. A Critical Bibliography of French Literature. 4 vols. Syracuse: Syracuse UP, 1947–61.

Cassirer, Ernst. The Philosophy of the Enlightenment. Trans. Fritz C. A. Koelln and James P. Pettegrove. Princeton: Princeton UP, 1951.

Chas, François. J.-J. Rousseau justifié; ou Réponse à M. Servan. Neuchâtel: Favre, 1784.

Cioranescu, Alexandre. Bibliographie de la littérature française du dix-huitième siècle. 3 vols. 1969. Geneva: Slatkine, 1999.

Cohen, J. M., ed. The Confessions of Jean-Jacques Rousseau. 1953. Harmondsworth: Penguin, 1979.

Coleman, Patrick, ed. Confessions. By Jean-Jacques Rousseau. Trans. Angela Scholar. Oxford World's Classics. Oxford: Oxford UP, 2000.

Coleman, Patrick, Jayne Lewis, and Jill Kowalik, eds. Representations of the Self from the Renaissance to Romanticism. Cambridge: Cambridge UP, 2000.

Coleridge, Samuel Taylor. Selected Poetry and Prose of Coleridge. Ed. Donald A. Stauffer. New York: Random, 1951.

Conlon, Pierre M. Ouvrages français relatifs à Jean-Jacques Rousseau: répertoire chronologique, 1751–1799. Geneva: Droz, 1981.

Conrad, Joseph. *Victory*, Garden City: Doubleday, 1924.

Cranston, Maurice. *Jean-Jacques: The Early Life and Work of Jean-Jacques Rousseau, 1712–1754*. Chicago: U of Chicago P, 1982.

——. *The Noble Savage: Jean-Jacques Rousseau, 1754–1762*. Chicago: U of Chicago P, 1991.

——. *The Solitary Self: Jean-Jacques Rousseau in Exile and Adversity*. Chicago: U of Chicago P, 1997.

Crocker, Lester G. *An Age of Crisis: Man and World in Eighteenth-Century French Thought*. Baltimore: Johns Hopkins UP, 1959.

Davie, Donald. "Personification." *Essays in Criticism* 31.2 (1981): 91–104.

Davis, Michael. *The Autobiography of Philosophy: Rousseau's* The Reveries of the Solitary Walker. Lanham: Rowman, 1999.

de Man, Paul. *Allegories of Reading*. New Haven: Yale UP, 1979.

Dent, N. J. H. *A Rousseau Dictionary*. Oxford: Blackwell, 1992.

Derrida, Jacques. *De la grammatologie*. Paris: Minuit, 1967.

——. *Of Grammatology*. Trans. Gayatri Chakravorty Spivak. Baltimore: Johns Hopkins UP, 1974.

Diderot, Denis. *Essai sur la vie de Sénèque. Œuvres complètes*. Vol. 25. Ed. Herbert Dieckmann, Jacques Proust, and Jean Varloot. Paris: Hermann, 1986. 33–431.

Doppet, François-Amédée. *Mémoires de Madame de Warens, suivis de ceux de Claude Anet, pour servir d'apologie aux* Confessions *de J. J. Rousseau*. Chambéry, 1786.

Eigeldinger, Frédéric. *Des pierres dans mon jardin: les années neuchâteloises de Jean-Jacques Rousseau et la crise de 1765*. Paris: Champion-Slatkine, 1992.

Foucault, Michel. *Discipline and Punish: The Birth of the Prison*. Trans. Alan Sheridan. New York: Vintage, 1979.

——. *Madness and Civilization: A History of Insanity in the Age of Reason*. Trans. Richard Howard. New York: Pantheon, 1965.

——, ed. *Rousseau juge de Jean Jacques. Dialogues*. By Jean-Jacques Rousseau. Paris: Colin, 1962.

France, Peter, ed. *Reveries of the Solitary Walker*. By Jean-Jacques Rousseau. Harmondsworth: Penguin, 1979.

Franklin, Benjamin. *The* Autobiography *and Other Writings*. Ed. L. Jesse Lemisch. New York: Signet, 1961.

Gagnebin, Bernard, ed. *Les Rêveries du promeneur solitaire*. By Jean-Jacques Rousseau. Paris: Livre de Poche, 1989.

Gagnebin, Bernard, and Marcel Raymond, eds. *Les Confessions*. By Jean-Jacques Rousseau. Paris: Gallimard-Folio, 1995.

Gautreau, Jacques, ed. *Les Confessions*. By Jean-Jacques Rousseau. Paris: Bordas, 1984.

Gay, Peter. *The Enlightenment: An Interpretation*. New York: Random, 1968.

——. *The Party of Humanity: Essays in the French Enlightenment*. New York: Knopf, 1964.

Geoffroy, Julien-Louis. Rev. of *Réflexions sur les* Confessions *de J.-J. Rousseau*, by Michel-Joseph Antoine Servan. *L'Année littéraire* 5 (1783): 99–100.

Gouhier, Henri. *Les Méditations métaphysiques de Jean-Jacques Rousseau*. Paris: Vrin, 1970.

Goulemot, Jean Marie. "Literary Practices: Publicizing the Private." *Passions of the Renaissance*. Ed. Roger Chartier. Vol. 3 of *A History of Private Life*. Ed. Philippe Ariès and Georges Duby. Trans. Arthur Goldhammer. Cambridge: Harvard UP, 1989. 363–95.

Gourevitch, Victor, ed. *The* Discourses *and Other Early Political Writings*. By Jean-Jacques Rousseau. New York: Cambridge UP, 1997.

Grimsley, Ronald. *Jean-Jacques Rousseau: A Study in Self-Awareness*. Cardiff: U of Wales P, 1961.

Grosrichard, Alain, ed. *Les Confessions*. By Jean-Jacques Rousseau. Paris: GF-Flammarion, 2002.

Gusdorf, Georges. *La Découverte de soi*. Paris: PUF, 1948.

Gutwirth, Marcel. "A propos du 'Gâteau': Baudelaire, Rousseau et le recours à l'enfance." *Romanic Review* 80 (1989): 75–88.

Habermas, Jürgen. *The Structural Transformation of the Public Sphere: An Inquiry into a Category of Bourgeois Society*. Trans Thomas Burger. Cambridge: MIT P, 1991.

Hartle, Ann. *The Modern Self in Rousseau's* Confessions: *A Reply to St. Augustine*. Notre Dame: U of Notre Dame P, 1983.

Havens, George R., and D. F. Bond, eds. *The Eighteenth Century*. 1951. Vol. 4 of Cabeen.

Hazard, Paul. *European Thought in the Eighteenth Century*. Trans. J. Lewis May. 1954. Harmondsworth: Pelican, 1965.

Hollier, Denis, ed. *A New History of French Literature*. Cambridge: Harvard UP, 1989.

Howe, P. P., ed. *The Complete Works of William Hazlitt*. Vol. 4. New York: AMS, 1967.

Kavanagh, Thomas M. *Esthetics of the Moment: Literature and Art in the French Enlightenment*. Philadelphia: U of Pennsylvania P, 1996.

———. *Writing in Truth: Authority and Desire in Rousseau*. Berkeley: U of California P, 1987.

Kelly, Christopher. *Rousseau's Exemplary Life: The* Confessions *as Political Philosophy*. Ithaca: Cornell UP, 1987.

———. *Rousseau as Author: Consecrating One's Life to the Truth*. Chicago: U of Chicago P, 2003.

Klapp, Otto. *Bibliographie der frazösischen Literaturwissenschaft*. 38 vols. to date. Frankfurt: Klostermann, 1956–.

Kopp, Robert, ed. *Petits poèmes en prose*. By Charles Baudelaire. Paris: Corti, 1969.

Kors, Alan, gen. ed. *Encyclopedia of the Enlightenment*. Oxford: Oxford UP, 2003.

Ladurie, Emmanuel Le Roy. *The Ancien Régime: A History of France, 1610–1774*. Trans. Mark Greengrass. Oxford: Blackwell, 1998.

La Harpe, Jean-François de. *Correspondance littéraire*. 4 vols. Geneva: Slatkine, 1968.

Leborgne, Erik, ed. *Les Rêveries du promeneur solitaire*. By Jean-Jacques Rousseau. Paris: GF-Flammarion, 1997.

Lejeune, Philippe. *Le Pacte autobiographique*. Paris: Seuil, 1975.

Lévi-Strauss, Claude. *Structural Anthropology*. Vol. 2. 1973. Trans. Monique Layton. New York: Basic, 1976.

Magnin, Peggy Kamuf de. *The Cast of Helen: Metaphorical Woman in the Text of Rousseau*. N.p.: P. K. de Magnin, 1975.

Mansfield, Harvey C., ed. *The Prince*. By Niccolò Machiavelli. Chicago: U of Chicago P, 1985.

Mauzi, Robert. *L'Idée du bonheur dans la littérature et la pensée française au XVIIIe siècle*. 1960. Geneva: Slatkine, 1979.

May, Georges. *L'Autobiographie*. Paris: PUF, 1984.

———. *Le Dilemme du roman au XVIIIe siècle: étude sur les rapports du roman et de la critique, 1715–1761*. New Haven: Yale UP, 1963.

Mazarelli, Claire (marquise de La Vieuville de Saint-Chamond). *Jean-Jacques à M. S°°° sur des réflexions contre ses derniers écrits*. Geneva, 1784.

Melançon, Benoît, ed. *XVIIIe Siècle: bibliographie*. 105 numbers to date. 1992– <http://mapageweb.umontreal.ca/melancon/biblio.tdm.html>.

Monney, Jean-Jacques. *Jean-Jacques Rousseau: sa vie, son œuvre racontées en un siècle de cartes postales*. Geneva: Slatkine, 1994.

Montaigne, Michel de. *The Complete Works of Michel de Montaigne: Essays, Travel Journal, Letters*. Trans. Donald M. Frame. Stanford: Stanford UP, 1957.

Munteano, Basil. *Solitude et contradictions de Jean-Jacques Rousseau*. Paris: Nizet, 1975.

O'Dea, Michael. *Jean-Jacques Rousseau: Music, Illusion, and Desire*. Basingstoke: Macmillan, 1995.

O'Neal, John C. *The Authority of Experience: Sensationist Theory in the French Enlightenment*. University Park: Pennsylvania State UP, 1996.

———. "Jean-Jacques Rousseau." Kors 3: 477–81.

———. *Seeing and Observing: Rousseau's Rhetoric of Perception*. Stanford French and Italian Studies 41. Saratoga: Anma Libri, 1985.

Poulet, Georges. *The Metamorphoses of the Circle*. Trans. Carley Dawson and Elliott Coleman. Baltimore: Johns Hopkins UP, 1966.

Raymond, Marcel. *Jean-Jacques Rousseau: la quête de soi et la rêverie*. Paris: Corti, 1962.

———, ed. *Les Rêveries du promeneur solitaire*. By Jean-Jacques Rousseau. Geneva: Droz, 1967.

Riley, Patrick. *The Cambridge Companion to Rousseau*. Cambridge: Cambridge UP, 2001.

Roche, Daniel. *France in the Enlightenment*. Trans. Arthur Goldhammer. Cambridge: Harvard UP, 2000.

Rousseau, Jean-Jacques. *The Collected Writings of Rousseau*. Ed. Roger D. Masters and Christopher Kelly. 9 vols. to date. Hanover: UP of New England, 1990– .

———. *The* Confessions *and* Correspondence, Including the *Letters to Malesherbes*. Ed. Christopher Kelly, Roger D. Masters, and Peter G. Stillman. Trans. Kelly. *Collected Writings*, vol. 5. 1995.

————. *Les Confessions. Autres textes autobiographiques. Œuvres complètes*, vol. 1. 1959.

————. *Confessions, extraits*. Ed. Jean-Pierre Nérandan. 2 vols. Paris: Larousse, 1990.

————. *Correspondance complète*. Ed. Ralph A. Leigh. 52 vols. Geneva: Institut et Musée Voltaire; Madison: U of Wisconsin P; Oxford: Voltaire Foundation, 1965–98.

————. *Emile; or, On Education*. Ed. and trans. Allan Bloom. New York: Basic, 1979.

————. *Œuvres complètes*. Ed. Bernard Gagnebin and Marcel Raymond. 5 vols. Bibliothèque de la Pléiade 11. Paris: Gallimard, 1959–95.

————. *Les Rêveries du promeneur solitaire. Œuvres complètes*, vol. 1. 1959. 993–1099.

————. The Reveries of the Solitary Walker, *Botanical Writings and Letter to Franquières*. Ed. Christopher Kelly. Trans. Charles E. Butterworth, Alexandra Cook, and Terence E. Marshall. *Collected Writings*, vol. 8. 2000.

Rudé, George. *The Crowd in History, 1730–1848*. London: Lawrence, 1981.

Schinz, Albert. *Etat présent des travaux sur J.-J. Rousseau*. Paris: Société d'Edition Les Belles Lettres, 1941.

Schwartz, Joel. *The Sexual Politics of Jean-Jacques Rousseau*. Chicago: U of Chicago P, 1984.

Servan, Michel-Joseph-Antoine. *Réflexions sur les* Confessions *de J.-J. Rousseau*. Paris: Portets, 1822. Vol. 2 of *Œuvres de Servan*. 5 vols.

Showalter, English. *The Evolution of the French Novel, 1641–1782*. Princeton: Princeton UP, 1972.

Starobinski, Jean. *Jean-Jacques Rousseau: la transparence et l'obstacle*. 1957. Paris: Gallimard, 1971.

————. *Jean-Jacques Rousseau: Transparency and Obstruction*. Trans. Arthur Goldhammer. U of Chicago P, 1988.

————. *Largesse*. Trans. Jane Marie Todd. U of Chicago P, 1997.

————. *Le Remède dans le mal: critique et légitimation de l'artifice à l'âge des Lumières*. Paris: Gallimard, 1989.

————. "Rousseau sans peine et en cartes postales." Rev. of *Jean-Jacques Rousseau: sa vie, son œuvre racontées en un siècle de cartes postales*, by Jean-Jacques Monney. *Dix-Huitième Siècle* 28 (1996): 541–42.

Thompson, E. P. "Patrician Society, Plebian Culture." *Journal of Social History* 7.4 (1974): 382–405.

Transformations du genre romanesque. Ed. English Showalter. Spec. issue of *Eighteenth-Century Fiction* 13.2–3 (2001): 139–499.

Trousson, Raymond. *Jean-Jacques Rousseau jugé par ses contemporains: du* Discours sur les sciences et les arts *aux* Confessions. Paris: Champion, 2000.

————. *Jean-Jacques Rousseau: la marche à la gloire*. Paris: Tallandier, 1988.

————. *Jean-Jacques Rousseau: le deuil éclatant du bonheur*. Paris: Tallandier, 1989.

————. *Jean-Jacques Rousseau: mémoire de la critique*. Paris: PU de Paris–Sorbonne, 2000.

————. "Quinze années d'études rousseauistes." *Dix-Huitième Siècle* 9 (1977): 343–86.

————. "Quinze années d'études rousseauistes." *Dix-Huitième Siècle* 24 (1992): 421–89.

Trousson, Raymond, and Frédéric S. Eigeldinger, eds. *Dictionnaire de Jean-Jacques Rousseau*. Paris: Champion, 1996.

————. *Jean-Jacques Rousseau au jour le jour: chronologie*. Paris: Champion, 1998.

Vaughan, C. E., ed. *Political Writings*. By Jean-Jacques Rousseau. 2 vols. 1915. New York: Franklin, 1971.

Voisine, Jacques. "Etat des travaux sur Rousseau au lendemain de son 250e anniversaire de naissance (1712–1962)." *L'Information littéraire* 16 (1964): 93–102.

Voltaire. *Correspondence and Related Documents*. Vols. 85–135 of *Complete Works/Œuvres complètes de Voltaire*. Ed. Theodore Besterman. Banbury, Oxfordshire: Voltaire Foundation, 1968–77.

————. *Lettres philosophiques*. Paris: Garnier-Flamarion, 1964.

————. *Sentiments des citoyens*. Ed. Frédéric Eigeldinger. Paris: Champion, 1997.

Wade, Ira O. *The Structure and Form of the French Enlightenment*. 2 vols. Princeton: Princeton UP, 1977.

Waldinger, Renée, ed. *Approaches to Teaching Voltaire's* Candide. New York: MLA, 1987.

Warville, Jean-Pierre Brissot de. *Mémoires*. Ed. Claude Perroud. 3 vols. Paris: Piccard, 1912.

Wokler, Robert. *Rousseau: A Very Short Introduction*. 1995. Oxford: Oxford UP, 2001.

Wordsworth, William. "The Old Cumberland Beggar." *William Wordsworth: The Major Works*. Ed. Stephen Gill. New York: Oxford UP, 2000. 49–53.

Zerilli, Linda M. G. *Signifying Woman: Culture and Chaos in Rousseau, Burke, and Mill*. Ithaca: Cornell UP, 1994.

INDEX

Modern Language Association of America
Approaches to Teaching World Literature
Joseph Gibaldi, series editor

Achebe's Things Fall Apart. Ed. Bernth Lindfors. 1991.
Arthurian Tradition. Ed. Maureen Fries and Jeanie Watson. 1992.
Atwood's The Handmaid's Tale *and Other Works*. Ed. Sharon R. Wilson,
    Thomas B. Friedman, and Shannon Hengen. 1996.
Austen's Pride and Prejudice. Ed. Marcia McClintock Folsom. 1993.
Balzac's Old Goriot. Ed. Michal Peled Ginsburg. 2000.
Baudelaire's Flowers of Evil. Ed. Laurence M. Porter. 2000.
Beckett's Waiting for Godot. Ed. June Schlueter and Enoch Brater. 1991.
Beowulf. Ed. Jess B. Bessinger, Jr., and Robert F. Yeager. 1984.
Blake's Songs of Innocence and of Experience. Ed. Robert F. Gleckner and
    Mark L. Greenberg. 1989.
Boccaccio's Decameron. Ed. James H. McGregor. 2000.
British Women Poets of the Romantic Period. Ed. Stephen C. Behrendt and
    Harriet Kramer Linkin. 1997.
Brontë's Jane Eyre. Ed. Diane Long Hoeveler and Beth Lau. 1993.
Byron's Poetry. Ed. Frederick W. Shilstone. 1991.
Camus's The Plague. Ed. Steven G. Kellman. 1985.
Cather's My Ántonia. Ed. Susan J. Rosowski. 1989.
Cervantes' Don Quixote. Ed. Richard Bjornson. 1984.
Chaucer's Canterbury Tales. Ed. Joseph Gibaldi. 1980.
Chopin's The Awakening. Ed. Bernard Koloski. 1988.
Coleridge's Poetry and Prose. Ed. Richard E. Matlak. 1991.
Conrad's "Heart of Darkness" and "The Secret Sharer." Ed. Hunt Hawkins and
    Brian W. Shaffer. 2002.
Dante's Divine Comedy. Ed. Carole Slade. 1982.
Dickens' David Copperfield. Ed. Richard J. Dunn. 1984.
Dickinson's Poetry. Ed. Robin Riley Fast and Christine Mack Gordon. 1989.
Narrative of the Life of Frederick Douglass. Ed. James C. Hall. 1999.
Eliot's Middlemarch. Ed. Kathleen Blake. 1990.
Eliot's Poetry and Plays. Ed. Jewel Spears Brooker. 1988.
Shorter Elizabethan Poetry. Ed. Patrick Cheney and Anne Lake Prescott. 2000.
Ellison's Invisible Man. Ed. Susan Resneck Parr and Pancho Savery. 1989.
English Renaissance Drama. Ed. Karen Bamford and Alexander Leggatt. 2002.
Dramas of Euripides. Ed. Robin Mitchell-Boyask. 2002.
Faulkner's The Sound and the Fury. Ed. Stephen Hahn and Arthur F. Kinney. 1996.
Flaubert's Madame Bovary. Ed. Laurence M. Porter and Eugene F. Gray. 1995.
García Márquez's One Hundred Years of Solitude. Ed. María Elena de Valdés and
    Mario J. Valdés. 1990.

Gilman's "The Yellow Wall-Paper" and Herland. Ed. Denise D. Knight and
    Cynthia J. Davis.
Goethe's Faust. Ed. Douglas J. McMillan. 1987.
Gothic Fiction: The British and American Traditions. Ed. Diane Long Hoeveler
    and Tamar Heller. 2003.
Hebrew Bible as Literature in Translation. Ed. Barry N. Olshen and
    Yael S. Feldman. 1989.
Homer's Iliad *and* Odyssey. Ed. Kostas Myrsiades. 1987.
Ibsen's A Doll House. Ed. Yvonne Shafer. 1985.
Works of Samuel Johnson. Ed. David R. Anderson and Gwin J. Kolb. 1993.
Joyce's Ulysses. Ed. Kathleen McCormick and Erwin R. Steinberg. 1993.
Kafka's Short Fiction. Ed. Richard T. Gray. 1995.
Keats's Poetry. Ed. Walter H. Evert and Jack W. Rhodes. 1991.
Kingston's The Woman Warrior. Ed. Shirley Geok-lin Lim. 1991.
Lafayette's The Princess of Clèves. Ed. Faith E. Beasley and
    Katharine Ann Jensen. 1998.
Works of D. H. Lawrence. Ed. M. Elizabeth Sargent and Garry Watson. 2001.
Lessing's The Golden Notebook. Ed. Carey Kaplan and Ellen Cronan Rose. 1989.
Mann's Death in Venice *and Other Short Fiction*. Ed. Jeffrey B. Berlin. 1992.
Medieval English Drama. Ed. Richard K. Emmerson. 1990.
Melville's Moby-Dick. Ed. Martin Bickman. 1985.
Metaphysical Poets. Ed. Sidney Gottlieb. 1990.
Miller's Death of a Salesman. Ed. Matthew C. Roudané. 1995.
Milton's Paradise Lost. Ed. Galbraith M. Crump. 1986.
Molière's Tartuffe *and Other Plays*. Ed. James F. Gaines and
    Michael S. Koppisch. 1995.
Momaday's The Way to Rainy Mountain. Ed. Kenneth M. Roemer. 1988.
Montaigne's Essays. Ed. Patrick Henry. 1994.
Novels of Toni Morrison. Ed. Nellie Y. McKay and Kathryn Earle. 1997.
Murasaki Shikibu's The Tale of Genji. Ed. Edward Kamens. 1993.
Pope's Poetry. Ed. Wallace Jackson and R. Paul Yoder. 1993.
Rousseau's Confessions *and* Reveries of the Solitary Walker. Ed. John C. O'Neal
    and Ourida Mostefai. 2003.
Shakespeare's Hamlet. Ed. Bernice W. Kliman. 2001.
Shakespeare's King Lear. Ed. Robert H. Ray. 1986.
Shakespeare's Romeo and Juliet. Ed. Maurice Hunt. 2000.
Shakespeare's The Tempest *and Other Late Romances*. Ed. Maurice Hunt. 1992.
Shelley's Frankenstein. Ed. Stephen C. Behrendt. 1990.
Shelley's Poetry. Ed. Spencer Hall. 1990.
Sir Gawain and the Green Knight. Ed. Miriam Youngerman Miller and
    Jane Chance. 1986.
Spenser's Faerie Queene. Ed. David Lee Miller and Alexander Dunlop. 1994.
Stendhal's The Red and the Black. Ed. Dean de la Motte and Stirling Haig. 1999.

Sterne's Tristram Shandy. Ed. Melvyn New. 1989.

Stowe's Uncle Tom's Cabin. Ed. Elizabeth Ammons and Susan Belasco. 2000.

Swift's Gulliver's Travels. Ed. Edward J. Rielly. 1988.

Thoreau's Walden *and Other Works*. Ed. Richard J. Schneider. 1996.

Tolstoy's Anna Karenina. Ed. Liza Knapp and Amy Mandelker. 2003.

Vergil's Aeneid. Ed. William S. Anderson and Lorina N. Quartarone. 2002.

Voltaire's Candide. Ed. Renée Waldinger. 1987.

Whitman's Leaves of Grass. Ed. Donald D. Kummings. 1990.

Woolf's To the Lighthouse. Ed. Beth Rigel Daugherty and Mary Beth Pringle. 2001.

Wordsworth's Poetry. Ed. Spencer Hall, with Jonathan Ramsey. 1986.

Wright's Native Son. Ed. James A. Miller. 1997.